D1709689

Visible Cities

THE EDWIN O. REISCHAUER LECTURES, 2006

Visible Cities

CANTON, NAGASAKI, AND BATAVIA
AND THE COMING OF THE AMERICANS

LEONARD BLUSSÉ

HARVARD UNIVERSITY PRESS

Cambridge, Massachusetts
London, England   2008

Library of Congress Cataloging-in-Publication Data

Blussé, Leonard, 1946–
    Visible cities : Canton, Nagasaki, and Batavia and the coming of the
Americans / Leonard Blusse.
        p.   cm.—(The Edwin O. Reischauer lectures)
    Includes bibliographical references and index.
    ISBN-13: 978-0-674-02614-8 (alk. paper)
    1. Guangzhou (China)—History.   2. Jakarta (Indonesia)—History.
3. Nagasaki-shi (Japan)—History.   I. Title.   II. Title: Canton, Batavia,
and Nagasaki and the coming of the Americans.
    DS797.32.G836B58 2008
    950′.3—dc22   2007041328

In fond memory of Marius Jansen

Contents

Preface

To survey a historical period or a society by narrating a tale of the rise
and decline of one or two cities is a well-proven rhetorical device. It
has actually become a "biographical" genre both in fiction and in non-
fiction. More than any other kind of human settlement, cities, with
their critical mass, their comparatively free atmosphere, their multieth-
nic populations, and also their often exploitive nature, provide a wide
choice of subthemes for approaching the history of human society.
Fernand Braudel structured his epic study of capitalism by following its
rise via a succession of port cities—Venice, Genoa, Antwerp, Amsterdam, and ultimately London, where the modern world system took off.

   Shortly after I had been invited to teach Dutch colonial history and
Indonesian history as Erasmus Lecturer at Harvard University in
2005–2006, Wilt Idema, then director of the Fairbank Center for East
Asian Research, kindly suggested that I should deliver the Reischauer
Lectures during my stay in Cambridge. Having no idea what kind of
audience I would be talking to, I somewhat recklessly decided to put
off choosing a subject until I had crossed the great pond. It was actually
Rod MacFarquhar, who in the meantime had taken over the reins of
the Fairbank Center, who suggested that, given my Leiden academic
background, I should talk about cross-cultural encounters in early
modern East Asia. Because I had been involved in source-publication
projects about Batavia, Nagasaki, and Canton, I wondered whether it

would not be fun to get some mileage out of the useful but admittedly thankless task of editing such publications by comparing the trajectories of this urban trio toward the end of the early modern period. These port cities were connected not only by their trading links across the South China Sea but also by the fact that they were affected in one way or another by the global transformations of the late eighteenth century. Different cultural backgrounds notwithstanding, all three happened to harbor Dutch and Fujianese expatriate communities.

Thanks to the diaries of Dutch East India Company servants who were resident in the three ports, we are comparatively well informed about daily life there. Curiously enough, no one has used this material before to draw comparisons and point out the similarities or differences between these emporiums, which operated as the windows on the world for Qing China, Tokugawa Japan, and Dutch-controlled Java. When additional research reminded me that American seafarers began frequenting the three cities in the last decades of the eighteenth century, the decision was readily made to address the ups and downs of these three China Sea ports during the rather chaotic and interesting period at the end of the 1700s. I found in the Peabody Essex Museum of Salem, Massachusetts, a surprisingly rich supply of historical visual material with which to illustrate my lectures.

Planning a marathon of three successive lectures forces one to come up with a balanced and well-timed menu in order to feed the audience with information in easily digestible chunks. I attempted to reach that goal by shamelessly copying the "Braudelian" feast—whetting the appetite with a taste of the long-term perspective, serving a main course of conjunctural developments, and finishing with the *faits et gestes* of individuals as the refreshing dessert. That schema has been preserved in this volume. The first chapter provides the broad outlines of the developments in the China Sea after China, Japan, and the Indonesian Archipelago witnessed epochal regime changes in the early seventeenth century. In the second chapter, the diverging trajectories of the three ports are followed through the eighteenth century, and in the final chapter I take the liberty of following the adventures of several colorful individuals who portray different characteristics of the era in which they lived.

With its unique library facilities and vibrant intellectual life, Harvard University offers unequalled opportunities for research and teaching.

My wife, Madelon, and I were privileged to be given the opportunity to teach in a back-to-back appointment in the History Department and thus to connect with the department's students and staff. That feeling of being a full member of the group was reinforced by our stay in Adams House. We gratefully remember the hospitality of Sean and Judith Palfrey at that wonderful establishment, which, thanks to the mysterious powers of its inhabitants and its able staff, stands apart as the most artistic house, with the most exotic habitués (Norman Shapiro and Yon Lee), and the best kitchen at Harvard. When our university ID cards expired on 30 June 2006, giving us that tactful but unmistakable nudge to return home, we were already prepared to go, because once the students had left at the end of the term, the soul of the house had seemingly gone on vacation too.

This is not the place to mention the names of all the friends we made during our stay, but I would like to thank the following people for the help they gave in one way or another while I was preparing these lectures: Rod MacFarquhar and Ron Suleski of the Fairbank Center; Holly Angel of the Asia Center; Peter Bol, Wilt and Eveline Idema, and Kuriyama Shigehisa of the Harvard-Yenching Institute; David Armitage, Bernard Bailyn, Philip Kuhn, and Joyce Chaplin of the History Department; and the staff members of Robinson Hall and the Widener and Harvard-Yenching libraries.

Arnout van der Meer and Cynthia Viallé helped me with collecting the more than one hundred beautiful color pictures that I showed during the talks, of which only a few are represented, in black and white, in this book. Matsukata Fuyuko and Haneda Masashi of Tokyo University sent the latest Japanese materials, and Dan Finamore, the late Jacques Downs, H. A. Crosby Forbes, and Frederic Delano Grant, Jr., shared with me their extensive knowledge about Canton. Felipe Fernández-Armesto, Eric Tagliacozzo, and Daniel Botsman gracefully commented on the three talks. Maritime historian and longtime friend Lincoln Paine went to great lengths to turn my "double Dutch" into decent English.

Finally I would like to thank Frans Spaepen, Peter Bol, and Wilt Idema of the board of the Erasmus Foundation, and Andrew Gordon, chairman of the Harvard History Department, for inviting us to and hosting us in Cambridge. May this book serve as a happy memento of what was a very rewarding experience for both Madelon and me.

Visible Cities

✑ 1

Three Windows of Opportunity

Navigare necesse est.

In the introduction to *Utopia*, which he dedicated to his learned friend Desiderius Erasmus of Rotterdam, Thomas More tells where and when he was inspired to write his philosophical romance. In 1516, when More was sent as an envoy to Flanders "to solve some differences of no small consequence in the English wool trade," he visited Antwerp. In that Flemish port city he was introduced to a certain Raphael Hythloday, "who seemed past the flower of his age; his face was tanned, he had a long beard, and his cloak was hanging carelessly about him, so that by his looks and habit I concluded he was a seaman." It turned out, however, that the weather-beaten man was a philosopher from Portugal who had accompanied Amerigo Vespucci on his explorations to the fabled new continent. A few days later More invited this globetrotter to the house of a friend with whom he was lodging, and after an exchange of civilities the three men sat down on a bench in the garden and started to discourse about the different customs and laws of European nations, and of those across the ocean. At the end of the afternoon More and his host were so enthralled by the wisdom and cosmopolitan knowledge of their visitor that they asked him to tell them after dinner all about the island called Utopia, "the best state of the commonwealth," which he had visited somewhere off the coast of the newly discovered American continent.[1]

It is not a coincidence that More situated his putative encounter with

1

the narrator of *Utopia* in Antwerp. In the sixteenth century strangers
from all points of the compass came to sell their goods at the famous
bourse in that city's commercial center. Trade was the bride around
whom everyone danced in Flanders. In Europe's port cities, policies
that favored and facilitated commerce found their expression in particular customs and institutions accepted by all those who traded their
wares. Commercial towns along the land and sea routes were indeed
the places where life was most cosmopolitan, where travelers from far
away met to exchange their goods and gossip. Port cities, situated by
the estuaries of rivers that reached inland like veins of ore into mineral-
rich rocks, were treasure troves for those who were curious about the
overseas world.

In Italo Calvino's novel *Invisible Cities*, the narrator Marco Polo,
squatting on a carpet at the feet of the great Kublai Khan in the imperial gardens of Cambaluc, tells his host a succession of tales about the
myriad forms of city life in his extensive empire, but, as the reader
gradually realizes, the serial story is a melancholic variation on one
theme: Messer Millioni's longing for his native town, faraway Venice.[2]
Kublai Khan knew that he would never be able to visit the cities on the
edge of his empire, but enticed by the Venetian merchant's tales, every
evening he asked for the story of another town about which to dream.

In later years, scores of artists would make the City of the Doges
probably the most portrayed port city of Europe. Even if northern Europe's kings did not all have a Venetian storyteller at their court, they
must have possessed at least a few Canaletto paintings to hang on
the palace walls and gaze at dreamily. Nowadays the enterprising tour-
ist, a Lonely Planet guide in his pocket, can reach any exotic destination in the world within twenty-four hours, or if he is a lazy arm-
chair traveler he can enjoy them by watching Discovery Channel on
television. The romance of world travel has been turned into instant-
consumption fare.

In this book, I would like to invite you to travel back in time to
visit three famous Asian port cities of yore: Batavia (Jakarta), Canton
(Guangzhou), and Nagasaki, a journey that used to take European travelers at least six to eight months. In the days of sail these three emporia
fired the imaginations of sailors and writers alike because of their extraordinary appearance and exotic attractions. Each has left a prodi-
gious legacy of archival material and pictures, which will enable me to

Canton in the second half of the seventeenth century. From Johan Nieuhof, *Het gezantschap der Neêrlandtsche Oost-Indische Compagnie, aan den grooten Tartarischen Cham, den tegenwoordigen Keizer van China* (Amsterdam, 1665).

act as your guide without having to fantasize too much about them.[3] I call Batavia, Canton, and Nagasaki "visible cities" because no other cities in eighteenth-century Asia were portrayed (and possibly even written about) as often as these ports, where East and West met in strikingly different but also similar ways. But before we embark on our real and imagined *Bildungsreise*, let me explain why I singled out these three early modern markets as the topic for the Reischauer Lectures.

The most obvious and immediate reason was the academic institution where I was to deliver the lectures, Harvard University, the alma mater of John King Fairbank and Edwin O. Reischauer. Those two intellectual giants provided for me, as for so many students of my generation, the gateway to the histories of China and Japan, traditional empires that, challenged by the West, developed in their own ways into the distinct world powers they are today. Reischauer and Fairbank's *The Great Tradition* and *East Asia: The Modern Transformation* formed the alpha and the omega of my undergraduate work at Leiden University, where every sinologist-to-be also had to learn about Japan.[4] Apart from his organizational genius, John King Fairbank is best remembered for his pioneering work on the treaty port system, *Trade and Diplomacy on the China Coast: The Opening of the Treaty Ports 1842–1854*. It is often forgotten that the Japan scholar Edwin O. Reischauer also liked to teach and write about ancient China and its maritime frontier. In one book that is particularly dear to me, the two fields fade into each other: Reischauer's *Ennin's Travels* narrates the harrowing adventures at sea of a Japanese monk in search of the Buddhist scriptures in China of the Tang dynasty.[5] So it would be fair to say that both scholars had some salt on their lips, and as it was the Fairbank Center that invited me to deliver the Reischauer Lectures, it was only fitting that my talks had to do with maritime matters.

The Maritime Sphere

The history of the maritime world of Monsoon Asia is a subject that in recent years has been somewhat neglected by scholars at Harvard University. Contemporary Japan and China's relations with Southeast Asia also do not seem to stir a particular interest among the political scientists of the Fairbank and Reischauer Centers. By focusing on two ports in the Far East and one in Southeast Asia, I hope to suggest that knowledge of China's and Japan's traditional relationships with the maritime sphere is crucial to our understanding of the global implications of Chinese and Japanese history in early modern—and contemporary—times. Indeed, if China and Japan contest each other's strategic and economic influence anywhere in the world, it is in the China Seas region, where both superpowers are vying for regional precedence.

The South China Sea became the starting point of the maritime "Silk Road" of the Indian Ocean more than a millennium ago, but it was not until the eighteenth century, when its port cities were directly connected with those in Europe, Africa, and America, that it turned into a crossroads for the global maritime trade. In the same way that Ayutthaya, Manila, and Pusan served in early modern times the political economies of Siam, Spanish-ruled Luzon, and Korea, the port cities of Batavia, Canton, and Nagasaki served as gateways to large portions of Java, China, and Japan. What makes these three ports particularly interesting to the historian is that they served not only as destinations in China's overseas trading network but also as nodes in the network of the largest Western trading power in the region, the Dutch East India Company, or Verenigde Oost-Indische Compagnie (VOC).[6] In all three markets, VOC personnel stationed at trading factories kept diaries or wrote reports about the local situation, and their writings about port life are unequalled in detail and volume by any other contemporary source materials.[7] As a result, we are provided with abundant archival sources that thus far have been tapped only sparingly.[8]

Situated on the Pearl River, Guangzhou has served for almost two millennia as the maritime gateway to the Chinese empire. In the seventeenth and eighteenth centuries Canton, as it was then known in the West, became, together with its satellite Macao, the port of call for foreign merchants in the huge Qing empire.

Nagasaki, the port officially designated by the shogunal regime of Tokugawa Japan, famous for its strict border laws and its angst about keeping its own identity, played host for more than two hundred years to Chinese and Dutch merchants who, to the exclusion of all others, were allowed to trade on two small, man-made islands in the Bay of Nagasaki.

Batavia, designated as the rendezvous point for the ships of the Dutch East India Company's trading empire, lived by the grace of maritime trade. Ideally located near the Sunda Strait, the thoroughfare between Java and Sumatra that connects the Indian Ocean with the China Seas, Batavia sat as a spider in its web. While Canton and Nagasaki were the outlets of two more or less self-absorbed agrarian empires with rich but in many ways also suppressed commercial traditions, Batavia was established as the emporium of a vast maritime trading empire that fed on the regional economies of Monsoon Asia and provided Europe with Asian consumption goods for almost two centuries.

All three ports were relatively recent configurations in the millennia-old monsoon trade: the Canton-Macao tandem dates from 1567, and Nagasaki and Batavia were established as international ports of trade in 1571 and 1619, respectively. But the vicissitudes of Canton, Nagasaki, and Batavia cannot be properly understood without referring to the traditional Chinese world economy of which they were part, or to which they were so closely connected. The economies of China's southeastern coastal provinces, and in particular the business acumen of the merchants from Fujian Province, directly or indirectly served as the driving force for all trade in the China Seas. Fujianese merchants formed the large majority in the Chinese communities in Batavia and Nagasaki, and even the networks of Co-hong merchants, with whom the foreigners had to deal in Canton, also hailed from Fujian Province.

Last but not least, it was exactly in these three port towns that the Chinese, Japanese, and Dutch welcomed the first American newcomers to Asia in the 1780s and 1790s. The three decades that sit astride the eighteenth and nineteenth centuries formed in many respects a turning point in the regional history of East Asia—as they did worldwide—and that is why I have decided to let them mark the end of this study.

The Time Frame

In his book *Origins of the Modern Chinese State*, Philip Kuhn labeled the 1790s a period of crisis in China.[9] A series of popular rebellions erupted along the margins of the Chinese empire, in the frontiers of the west and along the coastal borders of the south. The Yellow and the Yangzi Rivers spilled out of their riverbeds, flooding extensive tracts of the central regions of the empire. Less visible to the eye but no less perceptible was the impact of China's enormous demographic expansion. In the latter half of the eighteenth century the population more than doubled, increasing from 140 to 300 million, causing such related phenomena as regional famines, internal migration, and the tipping of the ecological balance through deforestation. Finally, this period marked the transition from the by then senile Qianlong Emperor and his corrupt grand councilor, Heshen, to his successor, the Jiaqing Emperor, who, the felicitous name of his reign period (Prosperous Age) notwithstanding, faced the thankless task of clearing up the mess and, as it turned out, the nigh-impossible task of restoring order to his chaotic domain.

In Japan we see similar phenomena: natural disasters such as the eruption of Mount Asama in 1783 caused unprecedented rainstorms, floods, and crop failures. The so-called Tenmei Famine lasted from 1782 to 1787. Peasant rebellions occurred all over the country, at a rate of more than fifty per year. When Shogun Tokugawa Ieharu passed away in 1786, a new, austere policy of frugality and moral redress was introduced, which led to the further limitation of overseas trade.

In the Indonesian Archipelago the Dutch East India Company, which saw its hegemony challenged by shifts in the nature of maritime trade in Monsoon Asia, suffered tremendous financial losses owing to the Fourth Anglo-Dutch War (1780–1784), when many of its ships were seized by the enemy near the English Channel. When the Napoleonic Wars broke off Dutch shipping connections with Asia at the end of the

1790s, the VOC was declared bankrupt and its East Indiamen on the Batavian roadstead were replaced by vessels under neutral flags, among which the Stars and Stripes figured predominantly.

If we take a global view, this same juncture in time was a period of crisis brought about by two simultaneous revolutions, the Industrial Revolution and the French Revolution. In economic affairs, Adam Smith presented a new paradigm of free enterprise and predicted the end of mercantilism with its monopolies and chartered long-distance companies like the VOC. A new age of information was in the making, in which knowledge about and awareness of other great civilizations on other continents were brought to everyone's doorstep, if not to everyone's tea table, in western Europe.

Old regimes in Europe were swept away by the winds of political change when revolutionary France invaded its neighbors, including the Dutch Republic in 1795. In the early 1780s, Britain lost one empire in the Western Hemisphere and started building a second one in Monsoon Asia. And while this was happening, pioneers and sailors from the ever-expanding Russian empire and the newborn United States of America set out on long treks and voyages, and reached for the eastern rim of Asia.

Of course, these revolutionary changes worked out differently in terms of the speed with which they had an impact on the world, depending on place and circumstance. Around 1800 we witness significant changes in the maritime trade in the China Seas, including the lapse of almost two hundred years of Dutch control in the seas surrounding the Indonesian Archipelago, and a spectacular rise in piracy and the number of interlopers seeking new corridors of trade.

As early as the 1780s new policies were formulated in the European metropolis vis-à-vis overseas "possessions" in Asia. The relative political independence of the chartered East India Companies as rulers of trade in the East was checked by the home governments in London and The Hague. Within Monsoon Asia itself the trade monopolies of the East India Companies were challenged by the rise of local agency houses and shipping companies. Members of the emerging industrial entrepreneur class in England even persuaded their government to send a royal envoy, the Earl Macartney, to the Manchu throne in 1783 with coffers full of British-made goods they hoped to sell to the land of the 300 million customers.

The departure of the return fleet of 1657. Governor-General Joan Maetsuyker
sends off Commander Joan Cunaeus to the *Peerl*, flagship of the fleet. Artist: J.
Isings, 1940. Collection of KITLV (Royal Institute of Anthropology), Leiden.

In short, the turn of the eighteenth into the nineteenth century was a
period of global transition and changing overseas entanglements to
which the regimes of China, Japan, and Java were forced to respond.
The control mechanisms that were worked out or refined in Canton
and Nagasaki probably give more insight into the mindsets of the Chinese and Japanese empires—and, we might add, the changes in Western thought and ambition—than any study of the center of those empires would give us. Through the windows of Canton, Nagasaki, and
Batavia we can witness the advent of modernity.

Port Cities

Ports have continually captivated those engaged in historical research,
but ironically there is no satisfying definition for the concept of the
port city, even though historians have given these cities an important
role in global history.[10] Fernand Braudel, for instance, pointed out the
particular role that a succession of port cities has played in the development of the *économie-monde*, or the modern world system, as Immanuel

Wallerstein has termed it.[11] Almost twenty-five years ago, an Australian team under the late Frank Broeze and Kenneth MacPherson started a comparative research project on port cities around the Indian Ocean and produced two interesting collections of essays, *Brides of the Sea* and *Gateways of Asia*.[12] They did not aspire to formulate big theory and declared themselves quite happy should the case studies provide "building stones which individually and collectively may lead to a better understanding of the development, functioning and the historical significance of port cities throughout Asia, and ultimately throughout the world." This same kaleidoscopic vision underlies a Japanese research program on port cities that recently produced three volumes of case studies under the title *Minatomachi no sekaishi* (The World History of Port Cities).[13] Yet the subtitles of the trilogy—*Minatomachi to kaikyoku sekkai* (Port Cities and Seascapes), *Minato no topography* (The Topography of Port Cities), and finally *Minato ni ikiru* (Living, or Life, in Port Cities)—suggest Braudelian inspiration because they vary from *longue durée* perspectives to snapshots of daily life, *le temps du monde*.

My aim is more modest. I intend to discuss three port polities around one seascape within a rather limited time frame. Taking the port towns of Canton, Nagasaki, and Batavia as focal points of human activity around the China Sea Basin, I will compare the radically different and at the same time curiously dovetailing maritime polities of the Qing empire, Tokugawa Japan, and the Dutch East India Company in the second half of the eighteenth century. Before I do this, however, let us look at the geographic features and the *histoire structurale* of the China Sea region to see how during the fifteenth and sixteenth centuries certain patterns of trade developed that would decide the settlement patterns of the European newcomers to the area.

China's Maritime Frontier

The China Sea region is often portrayed as an annex to the Indian Ocean, to which it is directly connected by the Strait of Malacca and the Sunda Strait.[14] Hemmed in by the coast of the Asian continent to the west and a string of volcanic islands on the eastern side, closed off in the north by Japan and in the south by the Indonesian Archipelago, the shape of the China Sea region reminds one of an hour glass, with the Strait of Formosa forming its waist. So while the Indian Ocean is open to the east where it connects with the Pacific Ocean, the shallow, land-locked China Sea is basically an inner sea, or a "Chinese Mediterranean," as it has occasionally been called.[15] The lower part, the South China Sea, comprising the whole region surrounded by the Philippines, the Indonesian Archipelago, Indochina, and South China, is almost completely situated within the tropics, while the upper section, the North or East China Sea, surrounded by China, Korea, Japan, and the Ryukyu Archipelago, tends to have a more rugged climate.

In the old days of sail, all traffic in the China Seas was directed by the predictable monsoon winds that blow alternately from the southwest and northeast. This basically meant that Chinese junks setting out for the southern sea—the Nanyang, or maritime Southeast Asia—would weigh anchor around the lunar New Year and reach their destination three or four weeks later, and then return after the change of the monsoon in early June. Unlike in the Indian Ocean where, depending on the direction of the monsoon, many ports were inaccessible for months on end, cabotage was feasible almost all year round in the South China Sea, thanks to its indented coasts and myriad islands that offered shelter and anchorage.

Navigation on the China Seas in the summer months from July to as late as October was—and still is—a very risky operation, owing to the typhoons that ravage the area with winds blowing at speeds of more than sixty miles per hour. Skippers of Chinese junks returning home from overseas destinations in the Nanyang would therefore make sure to leave as early as possible in June so that they could make it home safely before the typhoon season set in. All this of course also applied to Western shipping in the area.

At the beginning of the sixteenth century, when they first encountered the Europeans in Asian waters, the Chinese fishermen and traders had been reconnoitering and sailing the South China Sea for almost a millennium. They sailed along two corridors leading southward and westward from China. The eastern trunk route ran via the Philippine Islands in the direction of the Moluccas, or Spice Islands, while the western route skirted the coast of South China and the island of Hainan, crossed over to the coast of Vietnam, and then forked at the coast of Cambodia, one route leading in a westerly direction into the Gulf of Thailand, the other southward toward the Malay Peninsula and from there onward along the coast of Sumatra to its terminus at Java.

In addition to geographical considerations and their effect on maritime traffic in the China Sea region, man-made factors influenced the patterns and rhythms of trade and set the China Sea region apart from the Indian Ocean. These included the particular institutional restraints that Chinese and Japanese imperial administrations exercised on overseas trade in the region. Although the impact of the so-called Chinese tribute system, which from the Chinese point of view represented a Chinese world order extending into maritime and mainland Southeast Asia, has been greatly overestimated, it cannot be denied that the momentous changes of dynastic regimes and the subsequent state-formation processes that occurred during the seventeenth century in both China and Japan had an enormous impact on the China Sea trade. At the beginning of the seventeenth century, just when the *haijin*, the maritime prohibitions that forbade Chinese private merchants to sail to overseas destinations, had lost their practical use in China, the Japanese started to apply such prohibitions to secure their coastal borders, and perfected their execution to a degree of which the Chinese could only have dreamed.

The Limitations of the Official Mind

China's seaside border and its overseas connections have been studied by historians mainly from the viewpoint of the "official mind" of the Chinese imperial administration. John King Fairbank's work on the tribute system is based on those foundations, and his students have more or less followed in his wake—with the exception of John Wills, perhaps, who in his more recent writings about Sino-Vietnamese relations admits the shortcomings of this approach.[16] As a result we are saddled with a very one-sided view of the past, largely built on presumptions about how affairs along the coastal border should be conducted, according to the central government, instead of what they were really like. The doyen of the study of early imperial China, Hans Bielenstein, in his recent publication *Diplomacy and Trade in the Chinese World, 589–1276*, reaches the same conclusion when he boldly states that "a tributary system centered on China did not exist."[17]

Little effort has been made so far to compare the imperial myth (with its particular ideas about "how the imperial order should be extended to the surrounding peoples") with the real situation along the maritime frontier. The central government was more concerned about keeping its own "Han rascals" (*hanjian*) from mingling with (*jieji*) or enticing (*gouyin*) barbarians than it was about the threat of barbarian incursions, even along the northern border, which was perpetually menaced by nomadic tribes. How persistent this attitude was can be seen in the lively correspondence conducted by the Qianlong Emperor during the visit of the Macartney mission to China. The emperor was not particularly concerned about the conduct of the red-haired barbarians—that could be taken care of with the time-honored ritual for dealing with visiting vassals—but he dreaded that Chinese traitors might conspire with the visitors and give them subversive ideas.[18]

Insufficient attention has been paid to the steadfast denial by the court of the realities of an increasingly widespread "informal" Chinese presence and influence in the Nanyang from the sixteenth century onward. "Out of sight, out of mind" is an apt saying when it comes to the problematic relationship between the imperial administration and Chinese entrepreneurs in Monsoon Asia during the Ming and Qing periods. Contrary to European expansion overseas, the Chinese flag did not follow the trade, and as a result the importance of this creeping overseas expansion and economic penetration, which adapted itself to local conditions wherever it went, has been underestimated and misunderstood in current scholarship. What bothered the Chinese authorities from the beginning to the end was not the foreigners themselves but the way in which foreigners might be taken advantage of by their own subjects and as a result create problems along the border.

It was not until the outbreak of the first Opium War in 1839 that the Manchu government woke up to the real threat posed by the West.[19] Until then, the imperial authorities had worried mainly about the uncontrolled exploits of their own subjects abroad, whom they labeled as "pirates" and "unruly elements," but not about the challenges that European expansion might pose to the Chinese world order. Always looking within, always concerned with such "internal security problems" as piracy and smuggling, they were simply unable to glean much information about what was going on abroad because, in contrast to the Tokugawa administration, they made no concerted effort to collect such information. This is how, around 1800, a Chinese mandarin explained why China's elite was almost totally ignorant about the over-

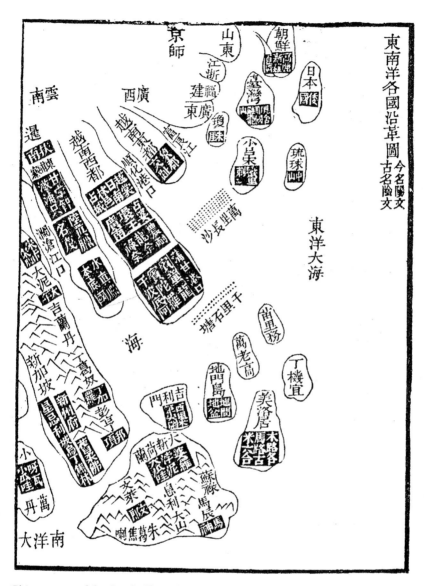

Chinese map of the South China Sea, 1852. From Wei Yuan, *Haiguo Tuzhi*
(Illustrated Treatise on the Maritime Kingdoms), 1844. Collection of the author.

seas world at the end of the Qianlong reign (I quote him with much
abbreviation): "We have almost no references to overseas kingdoms,
because they do not pay tribute and have no intercourse with our central kingdom . . . Our countrymen who trade abroad, merely think
about hunting after gain, and they have neither much knowledge of

books, nor any inclination or ability to record what they have seen. This constitutes a big problem."[20]

Policies toward Chinese Overseas Trade

In two pioneering articles written fifty years ago, the Chinese historian T'ien Ju-k'ang (Tian Rukang) was the first to draw attention to the importance of the Chinese junk trade with Southeast Asia during the seventeenth and eighteenth centuries.[21] Since then other historians have paid serious attention to different aspects of this early modern shipping network, thus gradually opening up new avenues of inquiry.[22] This research shows that early modern Chinese overseas trade expansion should be seen as resulting not from the tribute system of the imperial government, as many Sino-centric historians have maintained, but rather from the commercialization of the local economy and extravillage opportunities in the trade throughout China's southeastern coastal provinces.[23]

Before going further, let us look at the Chinese maritime trade network to see how this transportation system developed into the driving force that created and continued to shape overseas Chinese settlements in Southeast Asia in early modern times. To do this we should first look at the institutional background of China's overseas trade relations.

Official Chinese sources handed down over the past thousand years deal with metropolitan strategies toward the maritime frontier in a highly stereotypical manner. They tend to explain how China's relations with the overseas world were expressed in terms of the rituals connected to overseas tributary relationships, or in security measures applying to coastal defense, such as garrisons placed in strategic spots and the imposition of maritime prohibitions. While the administrative procedures for the reception of foreign traders in coastal cities remained remarkably uniform through the ages, the policies of the Chinese government toward its own subjects' sailing to foreign destinations were remarkably fickle. The tribute system that seemed ideal for channeling the comings and goings of foreign envoys and merchants to designated ports such as Guangzhou, Fuzhou, and Ningbo did not function well at all vis-à-vis the indigenous Chinese traders, whom the imperial administrators regarded as interlopers and infringers on imperial rule and order.

This situation became very clear when the Ming dynasty was established in 1367 after more than a century of Mongol domination. To gain full control over the border and do away with the Islamic traders at the coast who, during the *pax Mongolica*, had basically run China's overseas trade from coastal port cities like Quanzhou in Fujian Province—the well-known Zayton of Marco Polo—the first Ming ruler, Zhu Yuanzhang (1368–1398), forbade all private Chinese trade with foreign countries.[24] From 1405 onward, the Yongle Emperor (1403–1424), a usurper who desperately desired to establish his name and fame, sent seven large fleets under Zheng He, the "three jewels eunuch," via Southeast Asia to the Indian Ocean. The Chinese ships visited no fewer than thirty-seven countries. May it suffice to state here that as soon as overseas rulers, spurred by Zheng He's expeditions, started to send regular tribute missions to China, the Ming imperial government saw fit to withdraw from its overseas ventures and again reinforce the *haijin* maritime prohibitions for its own seafaring folk. Under the motto *Cun ban bu xia hai* (Not even a little plank is allowed to drift to the sea), stern warnings were issued forbidding Chinese private traders to sail to overseas destinations. Thus the tribute system that the early Ming emperors imposed on China's neighbors, ostensibly to achieve political stability by establishing proper relations between them and the Middle Kingdom, in effect prohibited their own subjects from linking up with foreigners.[25]

Although the maritime trade ban was intended to stem the swarming forth of Chinese private shipping, it produced a contrary effect. Defiant Chinese traders in the Malay Archipelago sought protection from local rulers and continued their activities as before. They even dressed up as "southern barbarians" and pretended to be tributaries from afar. The Ryukyu connection is also of interest in this respect. Fujianese families moved over to the island kingdom situated between China and Japan and not only became the main transporters of goods between China, Ryukyu, and Japan but also formed a link with Southeast Asia. Thus the interplay between legal (tributary) and outlawed (private) ventures kept the Fujianese maritime tradition alive. The crews sailing on tribute missions between Southeast Asia and Fujian basically remained "Chinese": they changed only in attire and in the flag they carried.[26]

Little effort has been made so far to dismantle imperial mythology with its particular ideas about "how the imperial order should be applied to the surrounding peoples" in the maritime sphere. Official policy toward Chinese trading overseas swung wildly from one extreme to the other, from the endorsement if not promotion of overseas trade during the Southern Song and Yuan dynasties to its total prohibition during the Ming dynasty. The widely divergent policies of the Ming court underscore this point.

At first overseas private trade was strictly forbidden, in order for the rulers to keep control over their own subjects and, of course, to ensure that only the throne reaped the profits of foreign trade, and only at designated gateways. In the long run, however, the court policy of monopolizing overseas trade through the tribute system turned out to be counterproductive and inefficient. While foreign trade in South China's main tributary port of Canton decreased to a mere trickle, there was a large-scale expansion of illicit overseas trade from the province of Fujian. This illegal activity, together with the arrival of the Portuguese, who were lured to China's coasts by Chinese smugglers, gave rise to a wave of piracy along the China coast during the 1550s.

Toward the Lifting of Maritime Prohibitions

By the middle of the sixteenth century, roving bands of Japanese and Chinese pirates, the *wo kou*, reigned in the East and South China Seas, from Japan to Luzon in the northern Philippines. Illegal trade and piracy networks spreading over the eastern seas had reached dramatic proportions. Efforts to enforce the maritime ban intensified, but it was observed that "the more strictly the prohibitions were enforced, the more the piracy increased." Consequently the Ming court was forced to revise its maritime policies.[27] The people of the southern coastal provinces, especially in Fujian, which depended on maritime trade, were desperate to have the trade legalized.

Thus in 1567 a two-tiered trade network with Southeast Asia, the so-called Dongxi-yang, or Eastern and Western Ocean network, was officially established for private traders from Fujian, the traditional home province of China's overseas traders.[28] Under the new regulations, the Fujianese were entitled to send out some 150 trading vessels along the eastern and western coastal routes of the South China Sea to destinations in the tropics at the start of each northern monsoon season. The southern Fujian port of Haicheng in the Bay of Xiamen, which under its former name, Yuegang, had been a smugglers' lair, was designated as a terminus for these trunk routes. Yet the government made it very clear that this outlet for Chinese shipping should remain off limits for foreign shipping. At the same time, the southern province of Guangdong kept its port on the Pearl River, Guangzhou, open as the traditional gateway to foreign tributaries arriving from the Nanyang. Ten years earlier local authorities had even allowed Portuguese merchants to set up a trading beach on a small peninsula in the estuary of the Pearl River, at Macao, from which they were allowed to trade in designated seasons with the merchants from Guangzhou. Thereby a pattern was created in which traders from Fujian Province were allowed to sail overseas while Guangzhou was kept open for foreign traders coming to China.

The Arrival of the Europeans

In one way or another, the European maritime powers that moved into the South China Sea at the end of the sixteenth century managed to capture a share of the China Sea traffic and attempted to adjust to the newly created transport situation: they either tried to sail to Guangzhou, as the Portuguese did, or they linked up to the Eastern Ocean route, as the Spaniards did at Manila, or the Western Ocean route, as the Dutch did at Batavia. Taking advantage of the embargo that the Ming government had imposed on all Sino-Japanese contacts, the Portuguese also opened a direct trading route between Macao and Japanese ports on the island of Kyushu.

Before I turn to the arrival of the Dutch in East Asian waters, let me summarize the operations of the first two European actors on the scene. The Portuguese settled down close to the outer end of the Xiyang, or western route, in the Strait of Malacca in 1511, and established fixed trading posts on the China coast at Macao in 1557 and in

Japan at Nagasaki in 1571. In this way they tried to gain control over the main thoroughfare between the Indian Ocean and the South China Sea and to tax the maritime traffic between the two. In addition, from their bases at Macao and Nagasaki they monopolized the trade between a Chinese market in want of silver bullion from Japan to grease its system of taxation, and a Japanese market that craved silks, porcelain, and other Chinese products.

The Spaniards situated themselves along the Dongyang, or eastern route, by establishing their headquarters in Manila in 1571, and they gave a further boost to the existing traffic by importing South American silver to the Philippines for the purchase of silk and porcelain from Chinese traders there.

The Newcomer

The Dutch East India Company, or VOC, owing to the expansive nature and inordinate scope of its activities in Asia, has sometimes been characterized as the world's first multinational company. It was founded in 1602 in the midst of the Dutch Republic's protracted war for independence from the Spanish crown. The Dutch States-General conferred on this long-distance company an extraordinary number of privileges, including the rights to wage war and to conclude treaties with "Oriental Princes and Potentates" east of the Cape of Good Hope. With such powers at its disposal, the VOC became an effective offensive weapon in the Dutch revolt against the crown of Spain and Portugal.[29]

By the time the first Dutch ships arrived in Southeast Asia, in 1595, the Chinese, Spanish, and Portuguese trading links had already been in full operation in the area for thirty years. Another two decades passed before the Dutch settled on an ideal location from which to direct their trading activities in the Indian Ocean, the China Sea, and the seas of the Indonesian Archipelago. This was Batavia, which Governor-General Jan Pietersz Coen, mastermind of the Dutch empire in the East, situated quite consciously on the western edge of the island of Java near the Sunda Strait, an important thoroughfare between the Indian Ocean and the South China Sea. Built on the ruins of the former kingdom of Jayakarta, which under the name of (Sunda) Kalapa already figured in Chinese sources as a port of trade, the Dutch intended Batavia to be

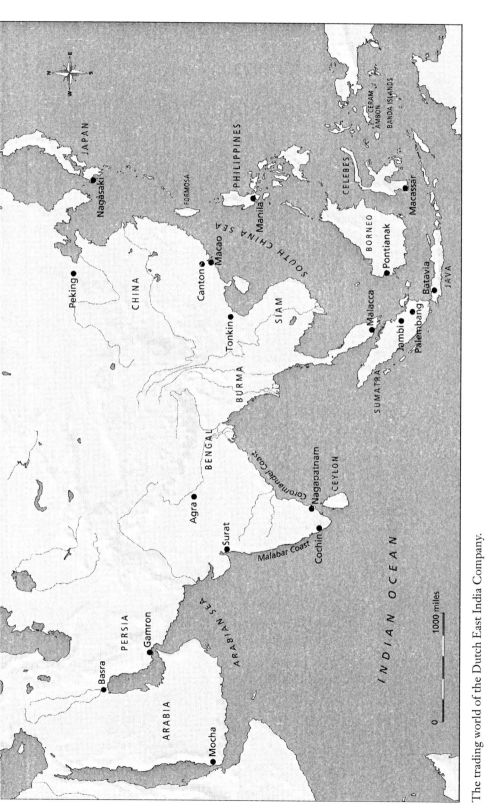

The trading world of the Dutch East India Company.

the terminus of the Chinese Xiyang route. For Coen there was no doubt that Batavia would have to depend on Chinese trading networks and Chinese manpower for its survival in the Indonesian Archipelago. More important, he believed that the opening of the China market held the key to any further success for the expansion of the VOC's trading networks in Asia.

Emulating the trading networks of the Portuguese Estado da India, the Dutch, who had far more ships, men, and financial resources, set out to create a self-supporting trading network in Monsoon Asia that would link the textile-producing regions in India with the spice-producing Moluccan islands and the enormously profitable silver-for-silk trade between China and Japan that was monopolized by the Portuguese. As this agenda was linked directly to the Dutch struggle for independence from the Spanish Habsburgs, a considerable amount of fighting occurred in the China Sea between the Spaniards and the Portuguese, on the one side, and the Dutch interlopers, on the other, until the signing of the Treaty of Westphalia in 1648.

The "Red-Haired Barbarians" in the Far East

The struggle for the markets of China and Japan was no less protracted and demanded constant adaptation and readjustment to local circumstances. The first VOC factory in Japan was established at Hirado in 1609 after a letter from the Dutch stadtholder Prince Maurice had secured a personal pass from the shogun. The Dutch (and the English, who followed a few years later) faced enormous competition. With their bases in Macao and Nagasaki, the Portuguese had acquired an almost unassailable position in the China-Japan trade.[30]

In the early decades of its existence, the Tokugawa shogunate (1603–1868) devised all kinds of stratagems to lessen its dependence on the Portuguese monopoly. Because Japanese shipping was not allowed in China, and Chinese vessels were still forbidden by the Ming imperial government to sail for Japan, the only way for the Japanese to acquire Chinese goods was to provide Japanese junks with shogunal passes, or *goshuin*, so that they could sail to destinations in Southeast Asia and there do business with Chinese traders. To this end, Japanese settlements, or *Nihon machi*, were established on Formosa, in Manila, at Hôi An and Tonkin on the Indo-Chinese coast, and in the capital of Siam, Ayutthaya.

The construction of a Dutch fortress at the entrance of the Bay of Tayouan (Formosa) in 1624 soon led to such friction with visiting Japanese traders that the Tokugawa *bakufu* declared a total embargo on Dutch shipping to Japan between 1628 and 1633. After this incident was resolved diplomatically, the directorate of the Dutch East India Company came to the conclusion that total subservience by its personnel in Japan to the local rules and customs was the only option, if the Company wished to continue to trade in that proud empire:

> Company officials . . . should above all be provided with modesty, humility, politeness, and friendship, being always very obliging in regard to the Japanese, so that their hearts shall in the end be won over to us. *Modesty* consists of prudent behavior and circumspection in all transactions; *Humility* means that one shall never raise jealousy with haughty actions towards this easily offended nation, but will always behave oneself as the lower one in rank; *Obedience* means that we should not resist their laws, without being too timid, or too indulgent, always trying to maintain the Company's rights in a discrete manner.[31]

These rules of conduct—along the lines of "When in Japan, do as the Japanese do"—became the guiding principle for all further action in the years to come and would serve the Dutch well, as we soon shall see.

Japan's wide-ranging overseas mercantile expansion, which occurred at exactly the same time that Dutch and English expansion in Southeast Asia began, was suddenly interrupted by the intervention of the *bakufu*. As part of his campaign to extirpate the Christian religion in Japan, where it was seen as dangerous and subversive, Tokugawa Iemitsu promulgated a succession of maritime prohibitions, or *kaikin*, between 1633 and 1636, bringing overseas Japanese traffic to an end and forbidding his (often Christian) subjects living abroad in the *Nihon machi* to return to Japan. In their rivalry with the Portuguese to gain part of Japan's foreign trade, the Calvinist Dutch only too gladly played up the Japanese hatred for the Catholic mission.[32] They assured their Japanese hosts that they, too, were involved in a ferocious struggle against the popish religion. As a matter of fact the Dutch East India Company presented itself to the shogunate as a nonthreatening alternative to the Portuguese. The fervent wish of the Dutch to replace the Portuguese

in the profitable China-Japan trade was fulfilled in 1639 when the Portuguese were banished "forever" from Japan.

Yet when François Caron, head of the VOC's Hirado factory, cau-
tiously inquired whether it would be a good idea for the Dutch stadtholder, Prince Frederik Hendrik of Orange, the "king of Holland," to
send an ambassador to the shogunal court in Edo to buttress trade relations, the answer was clear. The shogunal authorities felt there was no
need: "Why should their ambassador come to express gratitude for the
fact that the Dutch Company's merchants live and prosper in Japan?
Such business does not merit an ambassador. We only esteem kings and
potentates of substance, when they speak of royal business and not of
merchant business, when they request assistance in war or offer assistance. Sending another ambassador will only result in trouble."[33] In
other words, real ambassadors spoke about royal matters and not about
trade. This response reflected the full submission of the Dutch merchants to the state's regulations.

The true test came in 1640 when the shogun issued a decree that the
Dutch warehouses in Hirado should be razed, and ordered the Dutch
to move to the small island of Deshima in the Bay of Nagasaki, where
the Portuguese had been living. The shogun had been informed that
the Hollanders had had the insolence to engrave a Christian date, *Anno
Domini 1639*, on the gable of their newly built storehouse. Upon re-
ceiving this order, Caron replied, "What His Majesty faithfully ordered, we shall punctually execute [*kashikomatta!*]" and promptly ordered the building to be demolished. The Japanese official who had
transmitted the order sighed with relief when he saw it immediately
obeyed and is reported to have said: "This spares us considerable trouble and bloodshed." He had actually received orders that the Hollanders in Hirado should be cut down to size at the least sign of resistance
to the shogun's order.[34]

What was the direct effect of the implementation of these Japanese
maritime prohibitions? First of all, Japan's diplomatic relations with
Korea to the west and Ryukyu in the south remained intact, thanks to
the mediating function of the daimyo of Tsushima and Satsuma. The
Dutch, seeing new business opportunities, dispatched vessels to overseas ports that held more or less sizable communities of Japanese expatriates now cut off from their mother country. VOC ships were sent to
Cambodia, Hôi An, and Tonkin to carry on the trade of the Japanese

ships that had suddenly been interrupted. The same was true for the trade with Siam and Formosa, on sea routes where Dutch and Japanese merchant vessels had previously competed with each other. When the Dutch conquered Portuguese-held Malacca in 1641 and thereby gained control over the Strait of Malacca, the second thoroughfare between the Indian Ocean and the South China Sea, they became *the* dominant Western maritime power in the region.

In China the cards were shuffled in a quite different manner. No matter what they tried, the Dutch were unable to gain a foothold on the Chinese shore and initially had to follow the Japanese example and trade with the overseas merchants of the Chinese shipping network in ports throughout the Indonesian Archipelago, Siam, Cambodia, Hôi An, and Tonkin in Vietnam. Making no headway in this manner, Governor-General Coen opted for more aggressive methods to open the China market. In 1622 he dispatched a fleet of twelve ships to lay siege to Macao and thus make himself master of the China trade at Canton. When that gambit misfired, the Dutch built a base in the Pescadores Archipelago, hoping that they could plug into China's overseas trade from there. Instead, they were chased from the islands by a large Chinese invasion force in 1624 and withdrew to nearby Tayouan, where they built Zeelandia Castle, the second-largest Dutch fortress in Asia. During the thirty-seven years that the VOC ruled on Formosa, steadily extending its power over all of the island and bringing in large numbers of Chinese to develop the local agriculture, the Company grew into a regional power to be reckoned with, strategically situated, as it were, between China, Japan, and the ports of the various polities bordering on the South China Sea.

Angst over Imperial Overstretch

After forty years of intermittent struggle with the Portuguese, the Spaniards, the English, the Javanese, the Chinese, and the populations of the Spice Islands, it was time for the Dutch to draw up the balance sheet. Having first obtained a monopoly in the Moluccan spice trade, they had become engaged in nearly every important line of commerce throughout Asian waters by the middle of the seventeenth century. VOC merchants sent Indian textiles to the Indonesian Archipelago in exchange for spices and forest products, which they shipped throughout Monsoon Asia. From Chinese traders at Tayouan they purchased Chinese silk, which they sold for silver in Japan. Now that they had attained mastery over both thoroughfares between the Indian Ocean and the China Sea—the Sunda Strait and the Strait of Malacca—their position in Eastern trade seemed almost unassailable.

In the early 1620s the Company's directors, the Heren XVII, or Gentlemen Seventeen, who knew that all expansion was achieved at tremendous expense, were already cautioning the imperial strategist Governor-General Jan Pietersz Coen that the Company should avoid and excuse itself from costly warfare "if it is at all compatible with the preservation and safety of our estate. No great attention should be paid to the question of reputation or honor, which is often taken too seriously: in our opinion (for we are merchants) he has the honor who without doing injustice or violence has the profit."[35]

In a letter written in September 1633 to one of Coen's successors, Hendrick Brouwer, they further expanded on this theme and argued: "The best [way] is to submit to the laws of these Asian countries . . . we deem it to be much better for us to be subject to the laws and customs of those lands than to resort to arms, as long as it is tolerable and one can still trade profitably there."[36] From the beginning to the end, the managers and directors of the world's most powerful trading company were conscious of their limitations and afraid of imperial overstretch.

Confirmation for their concern was not long in coming. The promulgation of the *kaikin* edicts in 1636 had led to a veritable Dutch commercial boom in Japan, and within a few years the Far Eastern trade became "the principal trade in the Indies" for the Company, which served Formosa and Japan with, in those early years, up to twenty-two Dutch ships per year. As sole purveyors to the Japanese market, the Dutch were even able to contribute to the emergence of a separate "Japanese world order" alongside China's. By providing plenty of Chinese goods via Formosa, they softened the first blows of the *kaikin* edicts on the import sector of Japan's island economy and gave it time to adjust to the policies of the *bakufu* and eventually to reach an autarchic economic policy. Ironically, the Chinese trading partners of the Dutch now saw that the coast was clear for them to share in this booty, and they began to disregard the prohibitions of the Ming administration, which was occupied fighting a fierce battle with the Manchus along the northern frontier. Shortly afterward, silk deliveries from

China collapsed when civil war broke out in China and the Manchu invasion reached the production areas in the Yangzi Delta. This forced the Dutch to search frantically for other production zones that could supply the insatiable Japanese. First they were able to purchase silk in Tonkin, but soon they were sending their ships as far as Bengal. As a result, the VOC trade in the China Sea lost its closed-circuit character.

The Rise and Fall of the Zheng Empire, 1630–1680

In Chinese coastal waters the Dutch did not contribute to the stabilization of foreign trade as they did in Japan. By creating a disturbance in the maritime region, they were inevitably sucked up by the whirlwind of China's civil war, which raged for almost half of the seventeenth century. The frequent attempts of the Dutch to force open the China market, after they had established a stronghold on nearby Formosa in 1624, set in motion an unprecedented wave of smuggling and piratical activity in Chinese coastal waters that was amplified when the Dutch teamed up with Chinese smugglers along the Fujian coast.

Around 1628 one of the main allies of the Dutch, Zheng Zhilong, broke away and entered into the service of the provincial authorities of Fujian. Installed as a navy commander, he built up a sizable war fleet and succeeded in driving the Dutch out of the coastal waters. None the less, he worked out a modus vivendi with the Dutch on Formosa by promising them Chinese silks, porcelain, and gold for their trade with Japan, in exchange for silver and spices. In this way he gained firm control over all Chinese traffic with Formosa, even taking care of the large-scale dispatching of Chinese craftsmen, hunters, farmhands, and coolies to the Dutch-held island territory. By the early 1640s the Zheng clan was sending junks to Japan and Southeast Asia, and it thereby gained a virtual monopoly on southern China's overseas trade. This extraordinary, privileged position would not last long, however, because of the collapse of the Ming court amid civil war and rebellions. In this chaotic situation the Manchus finally saw their chance to cross the Great Wall, seize the throne in Peking, and proclaim the new imperial rule of the Qing dynasty in the summer of 1644.

A few years later, when Zheng Zhilong submitted to the newly established Qing court, his son, Zheng Chenggong (better known in the west as Koxinga), refused to follow his example and chose to remain loyal to the Ming court, which had fled to the south. Thanks to the huge profits that could still be reaped from overseas trade, he was able to recruit sufficient military strength to hold out against the Qing troops. Zheng Chenggong's main source of income was severely impaired, however, by a new ban on coastal and overseas trade issued by the Qing government in 1656. In 1661 the coastal population of China's southeastern provinces was even forced to move inland over a distance of thirty to fifty *li*—more than ten miles.

That same year, the Dutch were drawn into the Chinese civil war themselves. Before then they had been backing both horses, sending an embassy to the Manchu court in 1655 with a request to be admitted to trade at Canton even as they continued to trade with the Zheng faction in Fujian. Pressed by the advancing Manchu troops, Zheng Chenggong crossed over from the Chinese mainland to Formosa in the spring of 1661 and, after an eight-month-long siege, dislodged the Dutch from their strongholds there. It goes without saying that the loss of the Tayouan entrepôt in February 1662 wreaked havoc on the Dutch China Sea trade, which now became wholly focused on Japan.

Soon after the Dutch surrender of Formosa, the Chinese warlord started to plan a further expansion of his maritime kingdom to the Spanish-held Philippines. But all those plans came to naught with his sudden death in 1663. The Zheng clan held out on Formosa for twenty more years, until this last retreat of the Ming dynasty was finally incorporated into the Qing empire in 1683.

Sweeping Changes in Chinese Maritime Policy

The half century of civil strife in China between 1630 and 1680 saw the rise and fall of the Zheng maritime empire and, with that, first the opening up and ultimately the reincorporation of China's coastal region. During this period the maritime trading networks of Fujian Province created, under foreign overlords, sizable "Chinatowns" at Nagasaki, Manila, and Batavia, and—most important—incorporated Dutch-held Formosa into the Chinese world order. The picture that emerges from this overall sketch of the China Sea trade in the seventeenth century is that it was much influenced by the policies of the Tokugawa *bakufu*, which created niches into which the Zheng clan from Fujian and the Dutch newcomers could step, to bridge the voids

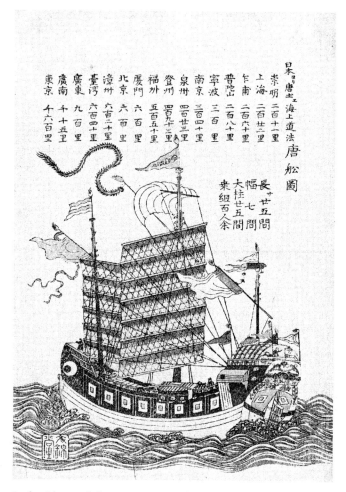

Chinese junk with travel distances. Artist unknown. Collection of the author.

in the China Sea traffic. Paradoxically, notwithstanding their protracted struggle against the Manchus, China's southern coastal provinces do not seem to have suffered during the war. On the contrary, when the Ming loyalists in Fujian were denied coastal shipping to the neighboring provinces, they relied even more on the overseas corridors and seem to have emerged with stronger links to their maritime environment than ever before.

During their thirty-year-long campaign against the southeastern coastal regions, the Manchus had resorted to the old tricks of issuing *haijin* and even evacuating the coastal population from the areas it con-

trolled in order to isolate their adversaries. But when Formosa, the last
bulwark of Ming resistance, was finally conquered in 1683, the imperial
court felt free to rescind the maritime prohibitions and to reinstate a
policy that struck a balance between its own security considerations
and the southeastern coastal regions' economic well-being, which had
to be preserved if piracy and smuggling were not to crop up again. The
central government had learned its lesson. Although the overseas trade
expansion that developed in the following decades basically followed in
the wake of the Eastern Ocean–Western Ocean network of the Ming
dynasty, it was no longer limited to Fujianese traders but open to private traders from all southern coastal provinces who wanted to join the
scramble.

Here we should dwell a moment on the momentous decision of the
Kangxi Emperor in 1684 to lift the ban on Chinese private trade again,
under the motto *Tongshang yumin* (Prosperous people through trade).
In his recently completed doctoral thesis, Gang Zhao points out that
the Manchus, whose homeland bordered on the Mongolian steppes,
China, and Korea, had a long history of favoring overland trade
because of their reliance on the trade network in northwest Asia.[37]
Nurhaci, the founder of the Qing empire, was deeply involved in the
transnational trade with China and Korea. There can be no doubt that
the Kangxi Emperor also saw the obvious advantages for the imperial
treasury of a flourishing overseas trade.

The Great Leap Forward of the Nanhai Trade, 1684–1717

The upsurge in the overseas traffic of independent Chinese traders after the pacification of the seaboard in 1683 was larger than either
the Manchu authorities, who had lifted the maritime prohibitions, or
the neighboring countries to which the traders sailed could ever have
imagined. Batavia and Nagasaki were the first overseas ports to bear
the brunt of this veritable tsunami of suddenly released Chinese shipping, although they dealt with it in two distinct ways.

Until the 1680s all attempts by the Dutch to establish regular trade
relations with China at Canton and other Chinese ports failed. They
had sent no fewer than three tributary missions to the Qing court in
Peking, all to no avail.[38] Now, with every monsoon season, Batavia was
suddenly served by large fleets of ten junks or more, which brought

ample supplies of Chinese merchandise. The Dutch were overjoyed, for this spared them the trouble of sending their own ships to the China coast, where they were subject to high tolls and exactions and the whims of the local mandarins. They contented themselves with being supplied by the Chinese shipping network, an arrangement that could lead only to more prosperity at the Batavian emporium. But soon, confronted with the annual arrival of twenty junks carrying thousands of traders and adventurers in search of work, the VOC authorities in Batavia became a bit nervous, especially when the town's Chinese headmen complained that they no longer could handle the influx. As a result, limits were imposed on the number of Chinese immigrants.[39]

In Japan, faced with the flood of Chinese merchandise into the market, the shogunate took drastic measures and imposed quotas on the almost one hundred Chinese junks that collected at the Nagasaki roadstead immediately after the trade prohibitions were lifted in 1684. The Chinese merchants in Nagasaki—there were soon almost 5,000 of them in this town of approximately 50,000 inhabitants—were confined to a *tojin machi*, or Chinese quarter, which was specially built for them not far from Deshima, and thus they lost their freedom of movement.

During this period of renewed overseas trade expansion, Amoy remained the main distribution center for China's coastal trade and the trade of the *huashang* (Chinese traders) along the Eastern and Western Ocean routes, but sailors from other southern ports, such as Guangzhou in the south, Shantou on the border between Fujian and Guangdong Province, and Ningbo in Zhejiang Province to the north, joined in the stampede to the Nanyang. The massive trade expansion to the Nanyang indeed provided the imperial treasury with the bountiful income it had hoped for, but the overseas emigration from the southern provinces and the frantic activities of adventurers abroad raised alarm in administrative circles at the Qing court in Peking. The dynamic, forward-moving maritime frontier of the south clearly was not the same as the Manchurian frontier in the north.

In 1717, the aging Kangxi Emperor again promulgated a ban on overseas trade in an effort to stem the unauthorized egress of migrants who were reputed to be turning the overseas regions into pirates' lairs. But the horse was already out of the barn: given the regional interests involved, it was no longer feasible to bridle the coastal regions with maritime prohibitions. The important maritime routes to Tonkin and

Cochin-China were reopened in the same year, and the trade with the islands of the Nanyang was resumed within five years.

How did these developments affect the position of Batavia and, more generally, the VOC's policies toward the China trade? When the Kangxi Emperor resorted to maritime prohibitions in 1717, the sudden stopping of trade played havoc with the Batavian economy, and although Macao took up some of the slack and the traffic was soon stealthily resumed, the Dutch authorities drew a lesson from this. In the future, the Dutch realized, such dependence on the Chinese network would have to be avoided at all costs.

New and Old Policies

At the same time, the Heren XVII, the directors of the Company in the Dutch Republic, were eager to reconnect with the China market. Tea and coffee were emerging as two important commodities for the trade with Europe. The Dutch brought coffee plants from Mocca, in Yemen, and after some experimenting in the Priangan area south of Batavia, the cultivation of Java coffee became a huge success. Tea cultivation and production was, however, a well-guarded Chinese secret, and for the moment tea could be purchased only at China's traditional outlet for foreign shipping, Canton. While the VOC was completely dependent on the tea deliveries to Batavia made by Chinese junks, the English East India Company and the Oostende Company of the Spanish Netherlands were sending ships directly to Canton, where they could select and purchase high-quality tea on their own terms. In 1727, the Heren XVII decided they would have to restore VOC shipping between the Netherlands, Batavia, and Canton so that they could compete on the same terms as their European rivals. Batavia remained the mainstay of the Dutch China trade. By providing Southeast Asian commodities for the Canton market, it contributed considerably to a healthy balance of trade. Lacking any exports that the Chinese wanted, other European buyers had to pay for tea with silver bullion specially shipped from Europe.

꒜ IN MANY RESPECTS the empires of China and Japan showed themselves to be immovable bulwarks before the first waves of European overseas expansion into Asia, in which the Portuguese and Spaniards took the lead in the sixteenth century only to be superseded by the Dutch in the seventeenth. There was a significant difference between Canton and Nagasaki. While Canton had served for almost a millennium as the designated port of call for foreign ships on the south coast of China, Nagasaki was literally invented as such a port in 1580, with the help of the Portuguese and the Jesuits. Batavia differed from both Canton and Nagasaki in being essentially an emporium situated at the periphery of the two mighty empires, and owing to its strategic position at a major crossroads of trade, it became the purveyor of tropical goods to China as well as Japan, via the Dutch and the Chinese shipping networks.

While the Chinese succeeded in keeping their coastal border free from the incursions of the Dutch "red-haired barbarians," they were not able to stem the spontaneous outflow of their own subjects to the Nanyang. Paradoxically, the strong imperial prohibitions on emigration and trade notwithstanding, the overseas expansion of Chinese adventurers, traders, and sojourners continued throughout maritime Southeast Asia. The maritime frontier of China was in all respects "leaking like a sieve." So strong and pervasive did the Chinese presence overseas become that the Dutch did not dare cut the Chinese shipping lanes, or corridors, to the Indonesian Archipelago (and specifically Batavia), for fear of killing the goose that laid the golden eggs.

The combination of the restrictive policies of the Japanese and Chinese states, on the one hand, and Chinese overseas enterprise, on the other, defined the parameters within which the Western colonial powers would gradually establish themselves in Southeast Asia and from there embark on their quest for the China market in the eighteenth century.

✐ 2

Managing Trade across Cultures

> In Chloe, a great city, the people who move through the streets are
> all strangers. At each encounter, they imagine a thousand things
> about one another; meetings which could take place between them,
> conversations, surprises, caresses, bites.
>
> ✐ Italo Calvino, *Invisible Cities*

By now the story line should be clear: in the course of the sixteenth and
seventeenth centuries, monumental changes occurred in the China Sea
region as a result of dynastic changes in China and Japan and the expansion of European maritime trade in Asia.[1] The interaction and en-
tanglement of these regional and global forces found their expression
in new port cities that came to serve this intercontinental traffic. The
perhaps unexpected *tertius gaudens,* or laughing third, in this narrative
is the network of private Chinese traders, which turned out to play
such a pervasive role.

Let us now see what Batavia, Nagasaki, and Canton looked like, by
what regulations and special measures the local authorities sought to
control and administer the foreign trade, and what commodities were
traded in these ports. The three ports may have been situated on the
rim of the same seascape, but they functioned very differently within
the states of which they were part. There was something particular to
each of these emporiums that should be pointed out before we look at
them in more detail. They were established by and modified according
to the requirements of three very different administrations: the commercial empire of the VOC, which fed on the intra-Asian trade; the
shogunal regime of Japan, which governed some 250 daimyo according
to a policy of *divide et impera;* and the Manchu empire of the Qing,
which, with a small warrior class and a collaborating Chinese literati-
elite, ruled 300 million Chinese peasants.

Canton has by far the longest credentials as a trading center, being the traditional gateway to the Chinese empire. Situated in the south-eastern province of Guandong, it may even be the oldest continuously functioning port in the world, as Professor Wang Gungwu recently suggested to me. In the middle of the sixteenth century the provincial authorities made special adaptations to the demands of Western shipping by allowing the Portuguese a trading beach in the Pearl River estuary, at nearby Macao. The Dutch and Spanish tried to secure trading beaches of their own in the first decade of the seventeenth century, but the Portuguese skillfully prevented this.[2] The port of Batavia was established in 1619 at the site of the former port of Jayakarta, or Sunda Kalapa. Its rise came at the expense of nearby Banten, which had served as the terminus of the Chinese and European trade on Java. And Nagasaki, as we shall see, was specifically put under Jesuit stewardship by the local daimyo to channel the Portuguese trade from Macao to his fief, at the expense of other ports in southern Japan.

All these ports were given a different "shape" at the end of the sixteenth and the beginning of the seventeenth century. This shape manifested itself most clearly in the measures taken to administer foreign trade. One of the characteristics of early modern states is the way in which they regulated their fiscal affairs with the relatively modest administrative apparatus available to them. Instead of collecting taxes, by and large they auctioned off this responsibility to so-called tax farmers or empowered chartered corporations to do the same.

In Canton an interesting shift can be perceived in the way taxes on trade were levied. Initially the Ming emperor competed directly with the Guangdong regional administration by sending his own eunuchs to the China coast to collect the proceeds from the import and export taxes. Under the Qing emperor, however, through a sequence of administrative adaptations, the court took incremental steps toward farming out the whole business of foreign trade to a group of licensed merchants, the Co-hong, while keeping a firm hand on the levying of customs duties, anchorage fees, and the like on in-coming and outgoing vessels by dispatching special officials for these functions.

In the Batavian case we see, under different circumstances, another typical early modern solution. The States-General of the Dutch Republic issued a charter to the United East India Company in 1602, under which the VOC had the exclusive rights to trade east of the Cape of Good Hope. Because of this monopoly, the Company levied its own import and export taxes at Batavia, but interestingly enough it farmed

out collection of many of the local taxes to Dutch and Chinese entrepreneurs.

In Japan, the management of foreign trade at Nagasaki was in many
respects more "hands-on" than in Canton and Batavia. After the *bakufu*,
the shogunal central administration, had intervened in an effort to control the prices of imported silk through the *pancado* or *itowappu* system
(see below), the city made the dramatic decision in 1698 to take the administration of all its trade, including the financial dealings, into its
own hands by establishing the Nagasaki Kaisho, or *Geldkamer*, as the
Dutch called it. This was a government-owned trading bank through
which all the financial affairs of the Dutch and the Chinese merchants
had to be settled.

In all three ports we see a large degree of government intervention
through an apparatus that was typical of the political structures of early
modern times. It was this profound urge to control business transactions that would render all three administrations unable to grapple
with the larger changes and shifts in the global economy, although for
obvious reasons the cracks in the system did show up earlier in Batavia
than in the others, because it was after all the headquarters in Asia of an
international trading concern.

The exclusive window ports of the Qing empire and Tokugawa Japan were politically subordinate to the tributary trade system of the
hinterland authorities in Peking and Edo, and were not necessarily
prime players in the processes of social, cultural, political, and economic development in the empires of which they were a part. Batavia,
however, served simultaneously as the bridgehead of the Dutch East
India Company's trading network in Asia and as the capital of an expanding colonial empire of territorial possessions in South and Southeast Asia. Colonial port cities like Batavia and Manila, unlike their
immediate pre-European predecessors, gradually gained control over
their hinterlands and created new political and economic orders that
were based on the subordination of the interior to the littoral.[3]

The Position of the VOC in Asia

The Dutch defined their own position in the region by distinguishing
three categories of administration for their establishments in Asia. First
of all there were the cities and the colonial possessions, such as Batavia,
Malacca, the Moluccas, and the coastal region of Ceylon, which they

had acquired by "conquest." Second, there were the often quite large settlements of company servants and their dependents in kingdoms where exclusive trade contracts with local officials guaranteed a privileged position in the trade of certain articles. The trading complex at Ayutthaya, the royal capital of Siam, for example, was one such factory.[4] Finally, there were the smaller compounds in Nagasaki and Canton, where the Dutch were allowed to trade in specific seasons and subject to extremely well defined and tightly controlled regulations imposed by the local authorities. In the early years when relations had not yet been properly sorted out, Governor-General Jan Pietersz Coen used to write his directors in Holland that the VOC was operating "among declared enemies and feigned friends."[5]

Situated amid a wide variety of port polities and extended territorial kingdoms and empires, the Dutch learned to tune in to the prevailing customs and practices of the Asian societies around them. Consequently, the VOC's representatives took part in all sorts of "exotic" practices and ritual behaviors. They wrote diplomatic correspondence in Malay, Persian, Portuguese, and Chinese; they were willing to kowtow in China and Japan; they patiently adhered to the elaborate rituals of the courts of the Mughal emperors and the rulers of Kandy and Mataram in Ceylon and Java; and they moved crablike over the floor at the Siamese court.

Once colonial Batavia had found its place among its Asian neighbors, the Heren XVII made it clear that attempts should be made

> to achieve voluntary, friendly traffic and a profitable trade, which is after all the principal reason for and aim of this company . . . when this has been done, one must go further and avoid and excuse oneself from all warfare where the location and the nature of the case makes this possible . . . no great attention should be paid to the question of reputation and honor, which is often taken too seriously; in our opinion (for we are merchants) *he has the honor who without doing injustice or violence has the profit.* This is unlike the considerations of princes and potentates, who often take the point of honor very seriously, yea all too seriously, but in our station it is a definite rule and dogma, which must be stated and obeyed.[6]

Company servants judiciously lived by these instructions and submitted to the laws and customs of Asian kingdoms where they were guar-

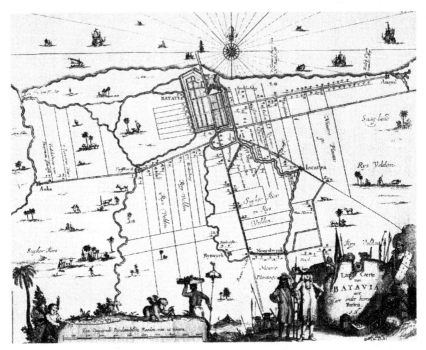

Map of Batavia and surroundings. Joan Nieuhof, *Joan Nieuhofs gedenkwaerdige zee en lantreize door de voornaemste landschappen van West en Oostindien* (Amsterdam, 1682).

anteed reasonable safety and protection. With the exception of the Portuguese, perhaps, no other Europeans ever became so much embedded in Asian ritual and custom as the Dutch of the VOC.

When the American historian Holden Furber in his comparative study *Rival Empires of Trade* characterized European activities in Asia during the seventeenth and eighteenth centuries as the "Age of Partnership," he meant to stress the relatively egalitarian way in which trade was carried out in the Indian Ocean. That being said, he admitted that we should not represent this "partnership" too romantically. The East India Companies sometimes were able to impose monopolies on indigenous populations, but it also happened—and this was most often the case—that Company servants simply had to follow the rules that Asian rulers imposed on foreign trade.[7]

Market traffic was based on mutual interest and competition, and was occasionally coerced by the threat of violence. The delivery to the European companies of certain products at a set price—pepper, for example—was arranged not through market transactions but in exchange for certain services, such as protection through firmly established treaties with local rulers. Treaties, capitulations, and contracts were looked upon by Asian rulers and European traders as a means of bringing about stable trading conditions.

Batavia's trade system was basically a redistributive one that came to depend on a tributary mode of production and exchange, a system the Batavian government gradually put in place within the Indonesian Archipelago during the seventeenth century through a series of treaties and contracts with local Javanese rulers. While goods flowed into the center of this maritime trading empire, Batavia was also a magnetic international emporium that attracted sojourners from many different ethnic backgrounds. These traders participated in and profited from the new economic order introduced by the Dutch colonial administration. In particular, the Chinese corridor that connected Batavia with the economy of south China fed the city a wide array of Chinese products and provided it with a constant flow of manpower. So well and regularly was the VOC served by this Chinese shipping link that in the late 1680s, the Company decided to stop sending its own ships to China, reserving them, instead, for the trade with Ayutthaya in Siam, Nagasaki in Japan, and the far-flung trade of the Indian Ocean.[8]

Queen of the Orient

Let us first imagine what Batavia looked like at the beginning of the eighteenth century, when it was still known as "the Queen of the Orient" and ruled an extended commercial empire of trade in the seas of Monsoon Asia. Established in 1619 as a typical colonial castle town, like its somewhat older precursors Portuguese Malacca (1511) and Spanish Manila (1567), Batavia was a mix of European planning and local traditions with old roots going back to earlier indigenous port polities. In this town founded and ruled by the Dutch East India Company, an extraordinary amount of space was allotted to warehouses and wharves. On average the Company annually sent some twenty-five ships to and from Asia and had about forty ships afloat on the Asian trading routes at any one time.[9]

The rectangular city was situated behind Batavia Castle, which commanded the seaward side. It was surrounded by a moat and a town wall with cannons on top not only for defensive purposes but also firing on the streets of the town itself in the case of insurrection. The Ciliwung or Kali Besar (Big River), elegantly lined by trees, cut the city in two and was crossed by bridges and canals. The straight, lined streets had double rows of trees providing shade and were brick-paved for the convenience of pedestrians. The houses of Batavia were built of brick in long rows like the town houses in Holland, but here they were often whitewashed to protect the interiors against the heat.

The merchant elite was originally housed in the imposing castle that overlooked the roadstead, while the town was designed in such a way that it included, next to the Dutch themselves, those ethnic communities on whose military assistance (free Christian burghers of Asian extraction, the so-called Mardijkers) and industry (the Chinese) its survival depended. This was in contrast to Manila, where strict segregation was maintained between the Spaniards and the Chinese settlers. At Batavia, Dutch, Asian Christians, and Chinese residents lived within the walls of one and the same town, served by large numbers of domestic slaves brought from within the Indonesian Archipelago and the Indian subcontinent.

In the so-called Ommelanden, the hinterland around the city, the Company allocated plots of land where the "martial nations" were concentrated in *kampongs* of their own—Balinese, Bugis, Madurese, and Ambonese. When called upon, these populations provided troops for military campaigns elsewhere in the archipelago.[10] After relations with the nearby port principality of Banten were stabilized in the 1680s and the surroundings of the town became secure, members of the merchant elite moved outside of Batavia's city walls and built themselves elegant mansions in the countryside.

Ships calling at Batavia first had to pass through a maze of islands—the Thousand Islands, or Pulau Serikat—before they arrived at the well-protected roadstead. Dutch East Indiamen, Chinese junks, and ships from other Western nations lay at anchor about a mile from Batavia Castle and the walled city, which were situated near the estuary of the great Ciliwung River. Wharves and chandlers were situated on islands, such as Pulau Onrust (Unrest Island), where everything was available for carrying out repairs. Two long piers extended from the land to channel the muddy waters of the Ciliwung River to the sea. Along this channel, smaller Indonesian vessels sailed to and from berths in the inner harbor, the Pasar Ikan.

In their overseas possessions the Dutch replicated all the well-developed municipal institutions of their burgher society in the home country, such as town halls, hospitals, courts of justice, churches, reformative institutions, and alms houses. Curiously enough, they provided comparable structures for Chinese institutions, such as the palatial dwelling of the Chinese *kapitein* (captain) that included an office where he met weekly with the other Chinese officers in town, and the well-equipped Chinese hospital. Directly outside the city walls stood Chinese temples and extensive cemeteries where the Chinese could bury their dead.

The town's extraordinary commercial orientation, its strong defenses, its eclectic cultural mix of citizens, and finally its neat representation of civic liberties and pride (real or imaginary) made Batavia appear, in the eyes of some of its visitors, to be a "Holland in the tropics," not least because of its system of canals lined by rows of trees and neatly built burghers' houses. Others looked beyond this European veneer and marveled at the Chinese component of the colonial town, idealizing the Chinese community as representing an alternative way of life and an example of social organization.[11]

Batavia was a complex multicultural community, especially when one realizes that other, perhaps less visible, cultural phenomena were also at work. The town had been founded on the ruins of the former port town of Jayakarta, and it sported many features of the indigenous port principalities of the region. The governor-general and the councilors of the Indies may have been housed in a castle at the water's edge rather than in a *kraton* (Javanese palace) in the middle of the town, but the ritual and ceremonial order that surrounded these gentlemen when they met with foreign visitors was of an almost regal nature. Every indigenous merchant visiting the town found that, as elsewhere in the archipelago, matters of trade were first of all dealt with by a *shahbandar*, or harbormaster, who not only provided translators but would also, in close cooperation with the captain of the Malays, provide for the writing of diplomatic letters to neighboring port principalities.

In the Malay world great ceremonial value was attached to the exchange of letters between rulers. The writing of such diplomatic correspondence was elevated to an art form in which the recipient had to be flattered in such a way as not to diminish the status of the sender himself. As the capital of a regional power, Batavia became involved in intensive diplomatic traffic with its neighbors around the Java Sea. Envoys from abroad were regularly received with pomp and circumstance and were ceremoniously accompanied to Batavia Castle, where the letter from their ruler would be presented to the governor-general and the councilors of the Indies who resided there. Many beautiful gold-leafed specimens of such diplomatic correspondence preserved in the VOC archives today bear witness to Queen Batavia's place among her indigenous neighbors and peers.[12]

Upon the departure of their fleets to Batavia every spring, the *yang-hang* security merchants of Xiamen (Amoy) never failed to send personal letters, accompanied by gifts, to the governor-general, idealizing him as the Ba Wang (King of Sunda Kelapa) who stood like a sturdy rock in the middle of the turbulent Southern Seas, and asking him to take care of the merchants they had sent: "Those living far away and Your neighbors proclaim their respect to you. Merchant ships sail to and fro. Batavia serves as an intersection for both land and sea transport. Thou, almighty Master, protect the lands of the Southern Seas. You maintain your laws and regulations. Your benevolence stretches out as far in the [Far] East."[13] Chinese shipping to Batavia was extraordinarily privileged. Unlike all other shipping, the junks from Amoy, on which the town relied so much, were not subject to import and export duties but merely had to pay preemption fees that released them from having their cargo searched. When the immigration of Chinese migrants threatened to become more than the local authorities could handle, all kinds of checks and balances were devised in collaboration with the Chinese leaders of the town, who were supposed to act as immigration officials—but with very little result.

Ethnic Strife

As I have described elsewhere, Batavia was as much a Chinese town as a Dutch colonial one. The Chinese lived there according to their own customs and under their own headmen, or captains and lieutenants, who in turn were subject to the Dutch colonial administration.[14] This seemingly harmonious arrangement was shattered by a dramatic event,

the *Chinezenmoord* (Chinese massacre) of October 1740, a massive po-
grom staged in response to a revolt and attack on the town by Chinese
vagrants who had lost their work on the sugar plantations. There can
be no doubt that the massacre of approximately six thousand Chinese then living within the walls of Batavia dealt a shattering blow to
the Chinese population in Batavia and to the urban economy. Adriaan
Valckenier, the governor-general who had presided over this carnage,
was removed from office and confined to a tower of Batavia Castle
while he awaited trial. When he passed away nine years later, proceedings against him had not even started, probably because nobody in
town had clean hands in the affair. To prevent the recurrence of such a
tragedy, however, all kinds of administrative measures were taken. A
separate Chinese quarter was built outside the town, and the administration of the Chinese community was further adapted to local needs
with the installation of the Chinese Council, or Kong Koan, which was
provided with its own office, the Gong Tang. There the *kapitein Chinees*
and his lieutenants would meet once or twice a week to administer justice over their own ethnic community and coordinate the administration of the sojourners, working in close collaboration with the Dutch
colonial authorities.[15]

Rather telling was the halfhearted reaction at the Chinese court when
the emperor received an apologetic letter from Batavia in which the
Dutch authorities informed him that they had deemed it necessary "to
render a true and detailed account, for fear that other people, jealous of
the flourishing trade that the Dutch enjoy in Your Majesty's empire,
may depict these incidents in false colors, with the aim of giving Your
Majesty the wrong impression of our lawful intervention, so that our
trade will be hurt and theirs will be favored." A confrontation occurred
at the Manchu court in Peking between groups of officials supportive
of the Nanyang trade and those opposed to it. One participant in the
debate pointed out that the Chinese who had been massacred had been
ignoring the emperor's order to return home and therefore deserved to
be punished according to Chinese law, although they were to be pitied
for their ghastly fate. Others remarked that the reinstatement of the
prohibitions against overseas trade would mean the loss of several hundred thousand taels in taxes and "would be even more harmful to the
traders who had built up stocks for the overseas trade."[16] At the end of
the debate, the emperor was advised by his court officials, "now that

The Chinese massacre in Batavia, 9 October 1740. Contemporary pamphlet.
Collection of Atlas Van Stolk, Rotterdam (no. 3597).

the king of Java [the Dutch governor-general at Batavia] repented and
wished to reform[,] . . . that the various barbarians in the southern
oceans be allowed to trade with us as usual."[17] The emperor really did
not care about his overseas subjects, who generally were referred to as
hanjian—traitors or renegades.

Environmental Decay

Slower in execution but even more deadly to the entire population of
Batavia was the collapse of the town's environment. By the end of the
eighteenth century, one out of three inhabitants died each year owing
to tropical illnesses or seasonal epidemics. That is an incredibly high
death rate—a whole city population every three years! This ultimately
forced the evacuation of the population from the downtown's torpid
canals to the healthier environs of the more elevated suburban area several miles inland.[18] Living organisms, including cities and nations, tend
to pass through life cycles, and Batavia was no exception. When James
Cook called at Batavia during his voyages of discovery when he needed

to repair his ship, one of his officers is supposed to have said of the town of desolated houses and gardens overgrown with weeds, that the mere thought of Batavia's unhealthiness would keep any other nation from attempting an attack.

Various explanations have been given for the transformation of this acclaimed urban settlement into an infamous death pit. Before the anopheles mosquito was identified as the true assassin only a hundred years ago, torpid, bad air—the word *mal-aria* says it all—was traditionally believed to be the killer. Recently another ingenious and quite convincing explanation has been advanced. It is now believed that the fish ponds laid out around the silted-up mouth of the Ciliwung River must have strangled Batavia because they provided excellent breeding grounds for teeming colonies of anopheles mosquitoes.[19]

To give you an impression of what it must have felt like to return to Batavia after several years of absence, let us read the words of Isaac Titsingh, whom we shall meet again later. After a long stay in Bengal in the early 1790s, he wrote that during his absence his friends had written him occasionally about the distressing decay of Batavia—

> but never could I have imagined how bad it really had turned, an impoverished and exhausted colony suffering more than ever under the fatal influence of an infected atmosphere . . . The town is partly abandoned, many of the most prominent houses are now occupied by third class people, the environs of the city still look prosperous, but the depression and despondency on the face of most people here shows how they are feeling . . . all this seems incredible to those who like me knew the opulence of Batavia 28 years ago and it surely makes their hearts bleed.[20]

Around the turn of the century the administrative center was moved from downtown Batavia to the higher ground of Weltevreden, and Batavia Castle was completely dismantled in 1807 on the orders of Governor-General Daendels, who was sent to the East to carry out Napoleonic reforms in the Dutch colonies. Today only a few buildings in downtown Jakarta remind us of the "Queen of the East," which by the end of the eighteenth century was already better known as the "Cemetery of the East." In hindsight one can see that the life cycle of

Batavia was closely tied to that of the East India Company itself. The
Company was dissolved in 1800, as was its headquarters in Asia soon
thereafter, although not altogether for the same reasons.

Another Climate, Another Country, Another City: Nagasaki

There was probably no more pleasing sight for the sailor approaching
the southwestern coast of Kyushu than the splendid spectacle of the
emerald mountains that emerged from the morning haze, soon to become crystal clear even at a great distance. Out of a deep blue sea dot-
ted with bobbing fishing boats arose isles covered with luxurious vege-
tation. In the background lay a landscape of hills, valleys, and small
bays with a scattering of fishermen's homes. This lovely scene would
show another face during the summer season, however, when it was
frequently battered by the destructive forces of the typhoons.

Tucked away behind this maze of islands and hills lay the sheltered
bay of the city of Nagasaki. Its approaches were indicated by the white
specks of huts on the hills that on closer scrutiny turned out to be the
protective housing for guns aimed at incoming and outgoing ships.
The shipping channel was lined with batteries all the way to Taka-
bokojima, or Papenberg Island, which marked the entry to the bay itself. (It was called Papenberg, or Papist Hill, by the Dutch, after the
shocking Japanese practice of throwing Christian believers down its
cliffs during the great Christian persecutions of the 1630s and 1640s.)
Surrounded by its pleasing hilly landscape, with the city of Nagasaki at
its end, the bay is about two miles in length and about half that in
width.

This beautiful land-locked bay provided a safe anchorage for local
fishing craft; the strangely shaped Japanese coastal freight vessels called
bezaisen; the brightly colored junks from China and ports in Southeast
Asia as far as Siam, Cambodia, and Tonkin; and the one or two Dutch
East Indiamen that lay at anchor there during the trading season. Approaching the city, the eighteenth-century visitor would discern on
the left a protruding, fan-shaped, man-made island with the name of
Tsukishima, or as it is better known, Deshima, and to the right the
more or less square Chinese quarter, the *tojin yashiki.* According to the
port city's original regulations, the rudder, cannon, and gun powder of
visiting ships had to be removed upon arrival, but over the years this

rule was abolished. All weapons, however, had to be locked up, and the only person allowed to keep his rapier was the head merchant on the island.

Nagasaki's story is an intriguing one.[21] Although its existence as a fishing village is said to go back to the first millennium, it was not until Portuguese ships from Macao started to visit in the 1570s that it entered the annals of world history. The local feudal lord, Omura Sumitada, happened to be a Christian convert, and to make sure that the ships of Macao would continue calling, he made quite an unusual decision. He ceded Nagasaki, lock, stock, and barrel, to the Jesuits on account of their instrumental role as interpreters and brokers in the port's trade with Macao. Alexandro Valignano, the Jesuit Visitor, found upon his arrival in 1579 a small settlement of only 400 houses, but in the years that followed that number increased sharply.

When in 1587 Omura Sumitada passed away, Toyotomi Hideyoshi, the warlord who would soon unify Japan, took possession of the town and promulgated his first anti-Christian laws. Jesuit property was confiscated, and the port of Nagasaki from then on was administered and defended in Hideyoshi's name by the adjoining fiefs of Arima and Omura. The Jesuit priests nonetheless soon regained control of the management of trade. Ten years later, matters came to a head again when Hideyoshi, suspecting the Spaniards and Portuguese of preparing an invasion, ordered the execution of a mixed group of Jesuits and Japanese converts, soon to be known throughout the Christian world as the twenty-six martyrs of Nagasaki. The Christian persecutions continued under Hideyoshi's successor, Tokugawa Ieyasu, but this does not seem to have adversely affected the continuation of the flourishing Portuguese galleon trade in Chinese silk for Japanese silver.

In 1636 the Portuguese were moved from the town to the island of Deshima. There they were confined until they were completely banished in 1639. Two years later it was the turn of the Dutch, who were relocated from Hirado, where they lived relatively freely, and restricted to Deshima, which became the Dutch residence for more than two hundred years. Deshima measured 600 feet in length and 120 in breadth, about the area of two soccer fields, and was surrounded on all sides by a palisade the height of a man. The island had two gates, one opening up to the bridge that connected it with the shore, and one on the other side, the *waterpoort*, through which goods were moved to and from the

Dutch ships that lay at anchor in the bay. During the two hundred years that the Dutch traders lived there, the right side of the island was mainly used for *kura* (fireproof storehouses) and the lodgings of the Company servants. Between the houses ran two streets, which were crossed in the middle by a third one leading to the gates. On the left side of the island there was a pleasure garden with the two-story house of the *Oranda Kapitan* (Dutch factory chief) in the middle. Adjacent to this was a vegetable and herb garden. The Company interpreters also had a very large house on the island where they would congregate during the trading season, and likewise the *otona* (wardens) and *dwarskijkers* (spies), who continually kept an eye on everything that happened on the island, had an office of their own.

This is not the place to discuss the early trade of Nagasaki in detail, but one point should be made about the price-fixing *pancado* or *itowappu* system, which the Japanese introduced to make the trade conform to local conditions and prevent large fluctuations in the price of silk. A group of specially appointed merchants from the large merchant cities of Sakai, Osaka, Kyoto, and Edo (Tokyo) would fix a price for the total consignment of silk brought to Nagasaki, and the whole lot would be sold under this contracted price. Although this intervention reduced the high profits of the Portuguese, at the same time it guaranteed them the complete sale of all their goods. This system was maintained off and on throughout the seventeenth century and really was the first in a long series of interventions that would characterize the Nagasaki trade. As Geoffrey Gunn has rightly remarked, almost all commercial transactions were mediated not by Portuguese or, later, Dutch practices but by local or indigenized institutions, at least at the point of purchase.[22] Arrangements of this type suited the visiting traders well, because they knew they would not be left sitting with part of their import cargo.

From the time they received their first trading pass, or *goshuin*, from Tokugawa Ieyasu in 1609, the Dutch did not have to pay any anchorage, import, or export dues in Japan. However, they were obliged to pay obeisance to the ruler on a regular basis. And so every year the *opperhoofd*, or chief factor, embarked on a *hofreis*, a court journey, to Edo in the company of a surgeon, a secretary, and a train of porters. During the trip the Dutch were given the same status as a daimyo. Along the way the travelers, who on Deshima had very little opportunity to mix with other people, had more freedom to meet and talk with the curious Japanese, who visited them at the inns along the road where they stopped for the night. The Dutch also used the opportunity to visit famous sites, such as the temples and shrines in and around Kyoto, and sometimes even to go to the theater in Osaka, with the inevitable result that the audience would gape at them instead of the actors. From the scarce personal correspondence preserved, one gets the impression that these trips to Edo offered welcome relief from the boredom of life on Deshima.[23]

The amusing stories about the court journeys made by the physician Engelbert Kaempfer, who accompanied the Dutch *opperhoofd* twice to Edo in the early 1690s, have been quoted over and over again, but the accounts of almost 120 other trips to the court that have now been published show that there was considerable variation over time in how the Dutch were received at court. Kaempfer emphasized the farcical atmosphere of the audience he attended, but this may have been closely related to the curious personality of Tokugawa Tsunayoshi, who loved to watch the exotic-looking red-haired barbarians from nearby and even had the *opperhoofd's* little son do a dance and sing a song for him.[24]

Having briefly explored how the Dutch lived on Deshima, it is now time to look at how the management of trade at Deshima was carried out. Here a general observation can be made. Throughout the seventeenth and eighteenth centuries, the shogunal administration strove to reduce Japan's dependence on foreign trade. It did so by taking some extraordinary monetary measures, first by forbidding the export of silver, then by depreciating the gold content of the *koban* coin to such an extent that it no longer made sense to use it as an export commodity, and finally by curtailing the export of copper. In 1698 the shogunal administration took over the financial administration of all foreign trade by establishing a commercial bank, the Nagasaki Kaisho, through which all financial dealings had to take place. While the Chinese government "outsourced" these kinds of financial services to security merchants, who were regularly driven into insolvency because of this practice, the Japanese *bakufu* chose to keep a tight rein on financial dealings to avoid any kind of bickering about unpaid accounts and so on.[25]

I have already mentioned the *pancado* or *itowappu* arrangement whereby the price of silk was set unilaterally by a consortium of Japanese merchants. In 1672 a taxation system (*shihō shōhō*) was introduced for ten different commodities. In 1685 this measure was replaced by

The frigates *Arinus Marinus* and *Ida Aleyda* at anchor in Nagasaki Bay, 1825.
Artist: Kawahara Keiga. Collection of Maritiem Museum Prins Hendrik,
Rotterdam.

the imposition of an annual ceiling of 300,000 taels on the annual trade
of the Dutch, and twice as much on that of the Chinese. (This was, of
course, in response to the sudden wave of Chinese junks that came to
trade after the maritime prohibitions in China had been lifted that
year.) On the instigation of *bakufu* adviser Arai Hakuseki, new regulations promulgated during the Shōtoku era (the so-called *shōtoku shinrei*)
limited the number of ships allowed to trade at Nagasaki to two Dutch
ships and thirty Chinese junks, and reduced copper exports to a maximum of 15,000 piculs (about 900 tons) for the Dutch and twice that
amount for the Chinese. Thus Japan's total copper exports were reduced to 2,700 tons. In 1790 the Kansei reforms curtailed the trade
even further, to a yearly quota of one Dutch ship and seven Chinese
junks and a maximum cargo of 6,000 piculs of copper for the Dutch
and double that amount for the Chinese.[26]

Although the volume of foreign trade was reduced, the Japanese
authorities continued to attach great importance to the comings and
goings of Dutch and Chinese vessels because it was only by interrogat-
ing their crews that they could gather information about the wider

world. News was systematically collected from Chinese visitors about developments in China and the Southern Seas. With the Dutch, this information gathering was even more institutionalized and refined. Upon the arrival of the Dutch ships every August, a group of interpreters would assemble to learn from the newly arrived Dutch factory head the news about the world, which they would write up as the *Oranda Fusetsugaki* (Dutch News Reports). Thanks to the research of Matsukata Fuyuko, we now know exactly how the intelligence was gathered and written down to be forwarded to Edo.[27] It goes without saying that the Dutch occasionally tried to manipulate this information, although they ran the risk that the Japanese might receive different information from the Chinese. The American and French Revolutions were reported, as was the French invasion of Holland in 1795, but this news was reported at a much later date to conceal the fact that the Batavian authorities were chartering neutral American, German, and Danish vessels when they could no longer dispatch Dutch ships.

This political information gathering cannot be dissociated from the remarkable progress made by contemporary Japanese scholars in their study of the West through the so-called *Rangaku*, or Dutch studies.[28] What started as early as the 1640s as a curiosity about Western medical practice grew during the eighteenth century into a profound interest in Western science and technology in general. In 1800, for instance, Shizuki Tadao, the pioneer who introduced the principles of Western linguistics to Japan, wrote an introduction to Newton's work in physics and astronomy on the basis of John Keill's *Inleidinge tot de waare natuuren sterrekunde* (Introduction to the True Natural Science and Astronomy) of 1741.[29]

Shizuki was the same author who invented the term *Sakoku* ("closed country") while translating Engelbert Kaempfer's chapter on the question of Japan's right to "stand off" from other nations and turn its back on international relations. It would not be until the beginning of the nineteenth century that the Japanese people would actually become conscious of the fact that, in keeping a distance from other nations, they were an "exception to the general human pattern." In Kaempfer's own words: "Hence the state and condition of the Empire [of Japan], such as it then was, the form of Government, as it had been lately established, the happiness and welfare of the people, the nature of the country, and the security of the Emperor in concurrence required, that the Empire should be shut up for ever, and thoroughly purged of foreigners and foreign customs."[30]

Thus what the Chinese were never able to achieve, the Japanese actually managed to carry out in their coastal waters. The shogunal administration fully controlled its military and economic affairs with a well-managed system of checks and balances. Any foreign ship that entered into Japan's coastal waters was immediately reported and searched; even the number of Chinese and Dutch ships permitted to visit Nagasaki was strictly limited. Relations with neighboring Korea were carefully managed by the lord of Tsushima, and the same went for the traffic with Ryukyu, which was supervised by the lord of Satsuma at Kagoshima in southern Kyushu. By the middle of the eighteenth century, almost all foreign import commodities had been replaced with Japanese products. The only remaining high-value export, copper, was subjected to a quota and sold to the Dutch at prices lower than on the Japanese market itself—a curious phenomenon, to say the least.

Canton, the Southern Treasury of the Emperor

The port city of Canton was situated on the banks of the Pearl River at quite a distance from the mouth of the estuary. This walled city, nicknamed *tianzinanku*, the "southern treasury of the Son of Heaven," had already served as a major port for foreign shipping for a millennium before the arrival of the Europeans. Its approaches were carefully protected against assaults from the sea by fortresses at various points along the river. I shall not enumerate in detail all the changes and adaptations made over the years to create the unique set of control mechanisms that regulated the port's trade with foreigners, the so-called Canton system. Authors like H. B. Morse and Earl Pritchard, and recently Paul Van Dyke in a revealing case study on the logistics of the port, have devoted whole chapters to these details; here it will suffice to sketch the general outlines.[31]

In the eighteenth century, ships never sailed all the way to Canton but instead dropped anchor at the Whampoa Reach, a roadstead approximately sixty miles upriver from Macao at the mouth of the Pearl River estuary, and some eighteen miles south of the city. It took the ships one or two weeks to reach this anchorage after they had engaged river pilots at Macao to guide them. They could sail only on the rising tide, and even then often touched the mud banks in the estuary with their keel. If there was no wind, some fifty sampans with oars were necessary to tow the East Indiaman to Whampoa. In 1784 there were no fewer than forty-five vessels lying at anchor there, stretching in a row three miles long![32] At Whampoa reach a Chinese Hong merchant (a security merchant) would assume responsibility for paying the necessary customs for a ship and stand surety for the orderly behavior of its crew. The attached Hong merchant arranged for the disposition of cargo and provided for the return cargo. He was in fact an "unofficial" official, through whom all communication with the port authorities had to be directed. Indeed, as Van Dyke has remarked, "This personal responsibility-management structure was a fundamental aspect of the control of trade from the beginning."[33]

Also indispensable were the *pidgin*-speaking linguists, or *lingos*, and their staff, who served as go-betweens in transacting the visitors' business with the *Hoppo*, or *Yuehaiguan jiandu*, the superintendent in charge of managing foreign trade for Guangdong Province. First appointed personally by the emperor in 1685 for a term of one year, the *Hoppo's* term was later extended to three years. These officials, often Manchus, ensured that they themselves would reap the most from this profitable position and were notorious for their venality. The *Hoppo* would personally visit an incoming ship and have it measured so that the port fees could be assessed accordingly. These port fees, consisting of various charges (too many to mention here), including the so-called emperor's present, varied between 3,000 and 7,000 Mexican dollars per ship. The formalities preceding the departure of the ships were no less strict and detailed. Only after all accounts had been settled was a Grand Chop issued, which served as laissez-passer for the passage down the river.

Canton's port fees were probably the highest in the world. After the duties had been paid, the unloading could begin, and the goods were transshipped into lighters, or "chop boats," which would forward them upriver for another twenty miles, all the way to the trade factories of the various East India Companies that were located outside the city walls.

This passage required expert navigational skills. Remarkable scenery unfolded before the eyes of the passenger as his dispatch boat, propelled by crimson sails and eight oarsmen, was skillfully maneuvered past hundreds of houseboats, tied to one another, belonging to the

Tanka, or Eggpeople, who spent most of their life on the water.[34] On the northern bank of the river our passenger would discern a riverfront block of thirteen two-story wooden structures, some with a national flag in front, extending altogether for more than half a mile. These were foreign factories, and it is said that they housed truly palatial interiors where the Company officers wanted for nothing but female company, which was strictly forbidden. William Hickey, who visited the English factory, wrote, "Each supercargo has four handsome rooms; the public apartments are in front looking to the river; the others go inland to the depth of two or three hundred feet, in broad courts, having the sets of rooms on each side, every set having a distinct and separate entrance with a small garden, and every sort of convenience."[35]

In the 1780s the East India Company factories of Denmark, Austria, Sweden, France, Britain, and Holland were situated next to one other, and according to the diaries of Dutch factory personnel—preserved, but sadly ignored by most historians—a lot of fraternizing went on among the personnel of different nationalities, even though they were competing in trade. The foreign merchants were allowed to stay in their factories only during the trading season. Once the ships had left, the supercargoes packed all their belongings and were off to nearby Macao, to enjoy the off season—February to the end of July—and take a rest. There they were allowed (after 1757) to rent houses where they could spend their leisure time with wives or concubines.

The Canton system, really an accumulation of procedures that over time had been refined and attuned to local conditions, may have looked rather confusing to the outsider. In reality, however, there was little to complain about because the foreigners ran a small risk. If a Hong merchant went bankrupt (which often happened), his colleagues would shoulder his debts and clear accounts with the foreign creditors. It is interesting that this Chinese court-enforced private guaranty of Hong debts to foreigners in Canton was the direct model for the "Safety Fund" established by the state of New York in 1829—one of the earliest bank-deposit insurance plans and a model for the Federal Deposit Insurance Corporation. It was cited in a letter to Governor Martin Van Buren from merchant and Safety Fund proponent Joshua Forman, who wrote:

The propriety of making the banks liable for each other, was suggested by the regulations of the Hong merchants in Canton, where a number of men, each acting separately, have, by the grant of the government, the exclusive right of trading with foreigners, and are all made liable for the debts of each in case of failure . . . This abstractly just principle, which has stood the test of experience for seventy years, and under which the bond of a Hong merchant has acquired a credit over the whole world, not exceeded by any other security, modified and adapted to the milder features of our republican institutions, constitutes the basis of the system.[36]

The whole range of regulations was aimed at keeping all interaction between foreigners and Chinese merchants as far removed from the imperial administration as possible. Contrary to the practice at Nagasaki, where prices were unilaterally set by the Japanese merchants and all the bookkeeping was actually in the hands of the government-run Nagasaki Kaisho, the Canton system left plenty of room for healthy competition among the Chinese security merchants who wanted to trade with the foreigners. Foster Rhea Dulles cites several participants in the trade who agreed that the Canton system worked well. The first American consul in Canton, Major Samuel Shaw, wrote that the trade in Canton "appears to be as little embarrassed, and is, perhaps, as simple as any in the known world."[37] These kinds of statements are confirmed by Robert Morrison's *Commercial Guide*, which states that "there was no port where trade could be carried on with such facility and regularity" as Canton.[38]

Tea Changes the World

Unlike either Nagasaki or Batavia, the trade at Canton was dominated by one product: tea. In early modern times probably no other commodity had such a sudden impact, both direct and indirect, on global trade in terms of consumption patterns, transport routes, and even politics. The unquenchable thirst of the Westerners, Europeans and Americans alike (in 1800 the Englishman consumed, on average, two and a half pounds of tea, sweetened by seventeen pounds of sugar a year)[39] dramatically changed not only the face of Asian history—the profits from the tea trade indirectly financed the English conquests in India—but also that of global history. After all, a shipload of Chinese tea thrown overboard into the waters of Boston Harbor set in motion a series of events that eventually led to the American War of Indepen-

dence. The intercontinental tea trade also led to an endless quest to restore the balance of payments, initially made mainly in silver, because
the West had little to offer to China.

New centers of distribution and exchange developed in Southeast
Asia, where tropical products were traded for opium and weapons so
that the English traders could provide the English East India Company
with sufficient funds for purchasing tea on the Canton market. Tea also
led incidentally to the mass production of opium in Bengal and the im-
portation of that "foreign mud" by the English and later the Americans
into China. The wealth of most of the old Brahmin families in Boston
was in fact solidly based on the tea and opium trade, because the two of
them became inextricably bound up with each other. Also closely connected to tea was porcelain, one of the oldest export commodities of
China. Protected on all sides by the large cargoes of tea, porcelain
could now be transported over long distances with little chance of
damage. When divers discovered in 1985 the remains of the VOC ship
Geldermalsen, which went down in the South China Sea in 1752, they
found that its cargo of porcelain was remarkably intact because the tea
cargo had cushioned it when the ship hit the seabed.

By the late 1730s, some 2,000 tons of tea a year were being shipped
to Europe by all European East India Companies operating in Canton.
When ten years later this amount had more than doubled to 5,500
tons, the first signs of market saturation became visible. The Dutch
East India Company, which transported the cheaper brands of tea, was
the first to feel the impact. The price of even the most select brands
declined and it became increasingly difficult for the Dutch to sell the
low-quality ones. Yet the VOC was helped by the continuous wars
in Europe. During the War of the Austrian Succession (1740–1748)
and the Seven Years' War (1756–1763), which took place far from the
Netherlands, the Dutch East India Company continued to send ships
to China while many of its rivals were temporarily incapacitated. After
the reorganization of the tea trade in 1757, when the directors of the
VOC installed the China Committee to run the tea trade directly from
Amsterdam, the Dutch company kept a market share of about 20 percent until the 1790s. Thanks to the help of independent British merchants trading between India and China, the so-called country traders,
the English East India Company held about one-third of the total
turnover.

Approval of the Commutation Act in 1783, whereby the English government reduced the tea tax from 119 percent to 12.5 percent, was bound to disrupt the European tea trade, which had largely supplied the English market via both legal and illegal ways. But because British shipping was not yet able to carry all the tea destined for the home market, the adverse effects of this change of policy were not immediately apparent. The real blow to the Dutch tea trade was the French invasion of the Netherlands, which made it well nigh impossible for Dutch ships to sail to and from Canton. Holland's loss was American shipping's gain.

So far I have been describing the reception of foreign vessels in Canton, but Paul Van Dyke makes an interesting point about the *huashang* network of this port in his recent study, for which he combed the archives of no fewer than seven East India Companies. Contrary to the impression given by earlier historians of the Canton trade, the data that Van Dyke has carefully pieced together show that Canton was also an important home port for junk shipping. The combined tonnage of the thirty sea-going junks based in Canton was equal to that of all the English ships at the port. And in addition to these, many junks hailed from other places, such as the rice-carrying junks from Siam. Tropical products like rice, wood, salt, coconut oil, animal hides, sugar, copper, lead, indigo, cotton, sticklac (a resin), horns, and ivory that were transported by junks from the Nanyang to Canton were largely intended for the Chinese market, but Van Dyke points out that some products, such as tin, lead, rattan, arrack, and sago were also used for packaging and stowage purposes on the foreign ships. These remarks bring us back to the subject of the previous chapter: the sadly underestimated tale of the Nanhai trade carried out by Chinese ships.[40]

The Weakening Grip of the Qing Administration, 1727–1840

In 1727, the same year in which the directorate of the VOC decided to restore the shipping link with China and send its own ships to Canton, Kangxi's successor, the Yongzheng Emperor, lifted all maritime prohibitions on Chinese overseas shipping, although he continued to have reservations about expatriates sojourning longer than one or two years in the overseas regions. Still believing in the principle of *dujian fangwei* (the forestalling of the growth of abuse by strict reinforcement of preventive measures), the emperor proclaimed:

> We believe that most of those who go abroad are malcontents. If
> We allow these people to come and go without taking note of the
> length of time they are abroad, they will increasingly lose their
> scruples, and leave their native places, and the number drifting
> around will be even greater. Hereafter, a time limit should be set,
> and if this limit is exceeded and they have not returned, then those
> people who choose to drift about in foreign places cannot be pitied. It is Our opinion that We cannot allow them to return to their
> motherland.[41]

New regulations regarding ship owning and limitations on and prohibitions of export items were introduced. One of the organizational
innovations was the introduction of authorized "ocean firms," the *yanghang*, which were licensed to engage in foreign trade, whereas the domain of the coastal trade of China was reserved for "merchant firms,"
or *shanghang*. The *yanghang* were supervised by security merchants
who were responsible for every ocean-going junk sailing to the Nanyang from Amoy, both for regulations of trade and the conduct of the
crew. Any person who wanted to travel abroad could do so only if kinsmen were willing to guarantee his return within a fixed period of time.

As I noted earlier, a series of deliberations at the court held in the
wake of the massacre of Chinese settlers at Batavia focused on the central issue concerning relations with Southeast Asia: whether to allow
or to prohibit private traffic. Among the defenders of the trading system, Qing Fu, the Manchu governor of the provinces of Guangxi and
Guangdong, was without doubt the most outspoken on the subject. According to this high official, another overseas trading ban was out of
the question. More than one hundred vessels from the southern maritime provinces were plying Southeast Asian waters, providing 500,000
to 600,000 people with trade-related work and generating an annual
inflow of 10 million taels in silver coins. Were the trade restricted, he
said, "the resulting situation would render people homeless and make
them wander from place to place, as there would be no food left for
thousands of persons because neither the merchants would have merchandise, nor would the farmers have produce."[42]

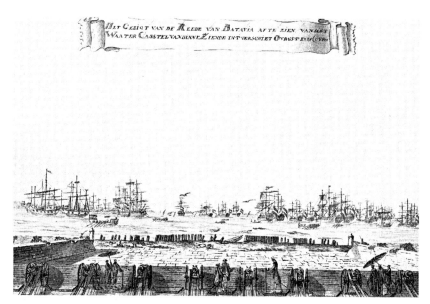

The harbor of Batavia seen from the "water castle," 1772. Artist: Johannes Rach. J. de Loos-Haaxman, *Johannes Rach en zijn werk* (Batavia, 1928).

All these developments underline the extreme dependence of China's coastal economy on the overseas trade. The moving in and out of people could no longer be stopped, even if the central government did see it as a great security risk. Merchants had not been allowed to return home if they stayed away longer than three or four years, but in 1754 the emperor relented and assented to a petition from Chen Hongmou, the governor of Fujian, who wrote as follows: "Because half the population [of that province] is depending on maritime trade for a living, those people who have remained a longer time abroad because they have not been able to sell their commodities or clear their debts in time should be welcomed home."[43] The strict regulations on the duration of residence abroad were slackened and the relatively free movement of people along the routes of the junk trade became possible.

In a rather futile attempt to counter the mushrooming of "China-towns" abroad, the emigration of Chinese women still remained restricted. However, Hakka women, who did not bind their feet, were often able to slip through the cursory examinations of customs officials. From this point on, migrants and sojourners became South China's most important export product. Carl Trocki has pointed out that this

led to the birth of a system of offshore production that included the
financing and transportation of settlers and the subsequent management of the trade in items produced and consumed by the Chinese migrants to Southeast Asia.[44]

Batavia Betrayed

In November 1752, Governor-General Jacob Mossel sent to the Heren
XVII his "Considerations about the intrinsic state of the Company," in
which he voiced his concerns about the marked decline of the Company's trade within Asia.[45] He believed that the Company's establishment in Canton could be instrumental in rectifying this unfortunate
situation because of the enormous profits to be made in the tea trade.
He conceded that many other European nations were also sending
ships to Canton, but he felt that the VOC's extended local networks for
collecting tropical products in the Indonesian Archipelago gave it a significant advantage over its rivals. Batavia could send regional products
such as tin, pepper, cotton, wax, spices, and other goods to Canton,
while European competitors in the China trade still had to pay for Chinese tea with precious metals.

In March 1754, the Heren XVII announced a complete reorganization of the VOC tea trade. They said that most of the tropical products
that the governor-general and council in Batavia proposed to sell in
China could be sold in Europe, as well, and perhaps at even better
prices. Adding insult to injury, the directors sneered that the Dutch
East India Company's European rivals, who sailed straight from Europe to Canton without idling at an intermediate station like Batavia,
shipped the new tea harvests to Europe much faster, and that consequently they put fresher tea on the market and commanded better
prices. They decided thenceforth to bypass Batavia, and took full control of this domain of trade by setting up an exclusive committee,
the China Committee, which from then on was authorized to manage
the direct trading link between the Netherlands and Canton. Thus the
High Government in Batavia effectively lost its grip on the VOC's
trade with China.[46] These reforms directly sealed the fate of Batavia,
because it would no longer serve as the terminus of the junk trade
in tea.

During the second half of the eighteenth century Batavia's position was undercut by yet another challenger. British country traders entered the South China Sea region selling opium, weapons, and Indian textiles wherever they could, in exchange for local products to sell on the Canton market. Circumventing the checks and balances of the VOC tariff system, they engaged in free trade with indigenous trading networks such as those of the ubiquitous Bugis, and the Taosug from the Sulu Archipelago.[47] The core of the Dutch trading network centered on the coastal towns of North Java remained intact, but traders on the periphery now turned toward the meeting points of the country traders and the *huashang* network of Chinese traders.

After the 1750s, the once flourishing Chinese trade that had formed the mainstay of Batavia's economy rapidly declined. By the end of the 1770s, the local authorities became thoroughly worried about the prospects of the junk trade, "which in the past was very considerable [in size] but now has gone in steep decline to the detriment of the local inhabitants." The governor-general and council even went so far as to address letters to the *yanghang* in Amoy, imploring them to send their junks directly to Batavia. The answer they received was telling. The Chinese shipping guilds made it clear that they could not afford to stay away from Johor, on the Malay Peninsula: "Otherwise they would have to give up their shipping enterprise itself for the simple reason that they did not know any other location where they could find all the timber necessary for the repairs of their junks and the construction of new rudders and masts." That was, of course, only part of the story. Navigation to Johor and other ports near the Strait of Malacca had fundamentally changed the flow of Chinese trade to the Nanyang and marginalized Batavia.[48]

Because many commodities from China were now distributed from transfer points around the Strait of Malacca all over the archipelago, even to places as far away as the east coast of Java, the tariff system of the Dutch East India Company was completely undermined. As Batavia lost its position as the terminus of Chinese trade to the free ports on the Malay Peninsula, the Chinese population in town sought other means of subsistence, and many moved into the hinterland. This trend was observed by Councilor of the Indies Isaac Titsingh. According to him, the almost complete disappearance of the junk trade not only affected all business in town but also forced the Batavian Chinese who had made a living from the China trade to close the doors behind them and move out into the countryside to start a new life there.[49]

Little could be done about these changes. As Governor-General De Klerck wrote as early as 1778, only in those regions where the Company reigned as *"heer en meester"* (lord and master) could it intercept interlopers. Elsewhere in the archipelago, in such ports of call for Chinese junks as Trengganu, Patani, Sangora, and even Johor, the Company simply could not intervene. By the 1790s the corridors of trade to and throughout Southeast Asia had branched out, giving rise to a number of smaller, less rigidly controlled ports from the Strait of Malacca to the waters east of Java, where country traders from India, Chinese merchants, Malays, Bugis, and Iranun from the Sulu Archipelago— traders, smugglers, and pirates—bartered Indian textiles, opium, and weapons for locally mined or commercially cultivated commodities like gold, tin, gambier, and pepper, or collected sea products, like trepang and shark fins, as well as tropical forest products, such as edible birds' nests, beeswax, camphor, bird feathers, and rattan, all of which had a place in the China market.

Yankee Traders to the Orient

When, during and after the years of the American Revolution, the Yankees saw their favorite area for trade, the West Indies, closed off by the British, they looked for other destinations, and the trade to the East Indies presented itself as an attractive alternative. On 22 February 1784, George Washington's fifty-second birthday, three months after the last British vessel had left New York, the *Empress of China* departed from the same port for the Middle Kingdom. The ship was fitted out on the initiative of the renowned entrepreneur and financer of the revolution Robert Morris of Philadelphia, "to encourage others in the adventurous pursuit of commerce." Morris had been able to select as leader of this expedition a famous war hero, Major Samuel Shaw, who was to become the American consul in Canton in the following years. A new American trade destination was born. In that same year, fourteen more American ships, from New York, Boston, Philadelphia, and Salem, would sail for the Indian Ocean and such ports as Mauritius, Batavia, Calcutta, Bombay, as well as to the northwest coast of America. The Yankee ships would sail to Mauritius, dispose of their cargoes there and take on freight for Canton, or purchase cotton at Bombay or Calcutta, pepper in Sumatra, sugar and coffee in Batavia, and seek such typical products for the China market as trepang and sandalwood in other smaller hubs of trade in Southeast Asia. Other ships would go hunting for seal near Cape Horn.

Vasco da Gama's supposed reply to the surprised local merchants of Calicut in 1498, when they asked him what he was looking for, was: "Christians, Gold and Spices." Major Shaw scribbled down in his journal *his* personal first encounter with a Chinese merchant as follows:

"You are not Englishman?"

"No."

"But you speak English word, and when you first come, I no can tell difference; but now I understand very well. When I speak Englishman his price, he say, 'So much, take it, let alone.'"

"I tell him, 'No my friend, I give you so much.'"

"He look at me, 'Go to hell, you damned rascal; what! You come here, set a price my goods?'"

"Truly, Massa Typan, I see very well you no hap Englishman. All Chinaman very much love your country."

Thus far [continues Shaw], the fellow's remarks pleased me. Justice obliges me to add his conclusion: "All men come first time China very good gentlemen, all same you. I think two three time more you come Canton, you make all same Englishman too."[50]

How true that observation was. In the wake of the English, the Americans would grow into the most formidable opium traders of the China coast.

The saga of the Yankee trade in the 1780s and 1790s has been studied mainly in terms of the trade with China, but that does not at all reflect the enormous expansion of American commerce all over Monsoon Asia and the Pacific.[51] According to the *Yuehai Guanzhi* (Gazetteer of Guangdong Maritime Customs) of 1839, "American ships were so numerous that they almost equaled those of England. Their ships, however, were rather smaller than the ships of other countries, and therefore could enter the port at any time, unlike the ships of other countries which can enter the port only in the eighth and ninth months

The *Franklin*, Salem, Massachusetts. Built in 1796, the *Franklin* was chartered by the Dutch in 1799 to sail from Batavia to Nagasaki. Artist unknown. Collection of Peabody Essex Museum, Salem (M11925).

of the year."[52] When Liang Tingnan, the writer of the gazetteer, was referring to the year-round presence of the Americans, he probably did not understand that the Americans came from all directions, including from the American West Coast, and thus were not so dependent on the monsoon as the Europeans.

We are still waiting for a historian who will piece together this commerce from all the various archives of the ports that were visited by these traders.[53] Here I shall make only a few general remarks derived from the studies of Latourette, Downs, Goldstein, and Dulles on the China trade. The ships from Philadelphia had the greatest tonnage at first, but soon New York took over the leading position; Boston developed trade especially with the American Northwest; merchants in Providence also started their Eastern trade with much capital; but best remembered are the many Asia-bound ships from Salem, Massachusetts.

In 1789 five of the fifteen American ships in Canton hailed from Salem, but after 1790 that share declined steeply. In effect only seventeen of the eighty-seven ships that Joseph Peabody sent to the Orient went to China; the remainder sailed to other destinations such as Mauritius, India, and Sumatra. By 1790 the China trade accounted for approximately one-seventh of America's imports. It is characteristic of the early years of the old China trade that the ships' records and the material objects that were brought home have been so carefully preserved. Many of these objects can be found in the Peabody Essex Museum of Salem, Massachusetts, which now also holds the treasures from the former Captain Forbes China Museum of Milton, Massachusetts. From the diaries of William Bentley we know that, around 1800, the inhabitants of Salem would dress up once a year in Chinese and Japanese attire and walk in a long, carnivalesque cavalcade through the streets of their small town.[54] In a recent Benjamin Franklin exposition in Philadelphia it was said that in Franklin's time, one out of five households in Philadelphia ate from China ware.[55]

Anybody who would like to know what it was like to sail in those days to the Orient should read that American classic *Delano's Voyages of Commerce and Discovery.*[56] Amasa Delano's adventures took him to China, the Pacific Islands, Australia, and South America from 1789 until 1807, when President Thomas Jefferson's Embargo Act is said to have brought American overseas trade to a sudden stop.[57]

Interestingly enough, the Dutch consul in Philadelphia, Pieter van Berckel, witnessed all these new developments and warned the States-General at The Hague that the Americans might well become formidable rivals and challengers to the Dutch East India Company's position in the Orient. He may have been right in predicting the enormous increase in the American presence in Asia, but little did he know that it would be the Americans who would bail out the Dutch in Batavia, Nagasaki, and Canton ten years later, when their country was invaded by the French and trade between Europe and Asia almost ceased.[58] The Napoleonic wars in Europe meant a tremendous loss for those countries that were not in the English camp, but provided a great boost for the commerce of the neutral American republic, until its self-imposed embargo under Jefferson in 1807 to 1809 and the renewed war with England that lasted from 1812 to 1815. A random look at the Batavian port register says it all: in 1804 the roadstead of Batavia was visited by ninety foreign ships: six Danish, two Spanish, two Portuguese, two French, two Swedish, two "Moorish" vessels, and no fewer than seventy-four American sailing ships!

Ups and Downs

This rough sketch of the trade situation in the China Seas at the end of the eighteenth century shows that while the Chinese junk trade reached dimensions it had never known in the past and served an extended network of overseas Chinese settlements, both Batavia and Nagasaki, erstwhile termini of Chinese overseas trade, had been downgraded to peripheral ports in the *huashang* network. In Nagasaki, this was the result of the Tokugawa *bakufu*'s deliberate policy of self-sufficiency, which sought to make Japan independent from the Chinese world economy. The Batavian administration, on the other hand, faced regional and global developments to which it could not formulate an appropriate response. The reorganization of the Dutch tea trade and the creation of a direct trading link between the Dutch Republic and Canton effectively eliminated the junk trade in Batavia, the most important source of income for its urban economy. The entry of English country traders into the Indonesian Archipelago and the China Sea region completely changed the rules of the game—or perhaps it would be better to say that, by interacting with the Bugis and Iranun networks, these interlopers did away with all the existing rules.

How different was the situation in Canton! By the 1790s, trade at this port was booming as never before. This period of irrepressible growth in the Canton trade represented the last triumph of the Qianlong Emperor, whose extensive campaigns to the west had almost doubled the size of his empire in his own lifetime. Yet this was no time for complacency. Although the Chinese administration at Canton had been very successful in shoving all trade with the foreigners into the hands of the security merchants, who were responsible for everything, the situation along China's southern maritime border ran out of control. For most of the period between 1790 and 1810, the coasts of Guangdong and Guangxi Provinces were ravaged by bands of pirates and smugglers to an extent not seen in ages.[59] This underscores once more a point that I made in the first chapter. The Manchu regime saw

the control of its own unruly subjects as its primary concern. Foreigners could be taken care of through the various checks and balances
of the Canton system; *hanjian* were an entirely different matter.

The emporiums of Batavia, Nagasaki, and Canton were created to
keep optimal control over the flow of trade into and out of East and
Southeast Asia. At the end of the eighteenth century, all three ports
met with a combination of internal and external challenges that threatened their status quo. Indeed, how utterly bewildering these developments must have been. Batavia collapsed because of the changing
fortunes in global trade, and Nagasaki's trade dwindled as a result of
national policy. But Canton experienced a meteoric rise thanks to tea, a
unique article of export that only China could offer to the world. This
success came at a cost for the Chinese people, however. The conquest
of Bengal gave the English East India Company the opportunity to tap
the local taxation systems of that vast region, although to do so it had to
raise huge armies, which by the end of the century numbered almost a
hundred thousand men. Through aggressive British army campaigns,
the Mughals' poppy plantations fell into the lap of the new rulers of the
Raj, who did not miss a chance to develop them and export their perni-
cious product in ever greater quantities to Southeast Asia and China,
ultimately throwing entire societies out of balance. How these stormy
developments led to the accumulation of huge private fortunes in India
and a flurry of accusations of corruption that shook even the British establishment in London is only too well known.[60]

It is indeed ironic that Britain, the nation that prided itself on having
first exposed the excrescences of the American slave trade (in which it
had been by far the greatest participant) *after* it had lost the American
colonies, from the moment that its so-called second empire in India
was taking shape, was engaged in the master planning of another kind
of enslavement in Asia: opium addiction. The story of how this created
all kinds of tension within the English community at Canton, between
unruly captains of the country trading vessels and the supercargoes of
the East India Company residing in Canton, has been told in detail by
Liu, Pritchard, and Morse.[61]

Last but not least, the French Revolution, and in its aftermath the
Napoleonic Wars, had a worldwide impact on trade. The Dutch were
all too aware of the tremendous upheaval caused by this revolution, but

it occurred far beyond the horizon of the Qing and Tokugawa governments—although both were informed about the rise of Napoleon. The
Dutch in Batavia were the only ones who saw what was coming and
tried to navigate through the Scylla and Charybdis of a faltering trading company and the occupation of their own fatherland.

3

Bridging the Divide

What is man that thou art mindful of him?
~ Psalm 8:4

Thus far we have seen how the persistently suspicious stance of the Chinese and Japanese regimes vis-à-vis the overseas trading ventures of their own subjects determined and shaped the ways in which the European traders entered the China Sea trade and ended up in the emporiums of Canton and Nagasaki. We have also reviewed the various administrative control mechanisms for overseas trade that were developed in the ports of Batavia, Canton, and Nagasaki, and observed how these were affected by shifts in global trade near the end of the eighteenth century.

In this last chapter we will look at human agency, what Braudel called "*le temps individuel*," the rapid rhythm of "individual" time, as experienced by persons living then. We cannot possibly get a feel for these three Asian port cities if we do not listen to the individual voices of those who visited them, and lived and worked there. How did Chinese, Japanese, and Dutch traders testify to the times in which they lived, and how did they reflect on the "human condition" in the ports where they worked and lived? Limitations of time and space force me to make some personal and highly subjective choices, which to some extent are also comments on and rebuttals of views that have been aired elsewhere in the literature.

I began the first chapter by referring to Thomas More, because it was really in his lifetime that European thinkers started to ponder other (non-Christian) cultures, what they had to offer and what they were lacking. The ongoing quest for an existing "Paradise on Earth" that was typical of the Middle Ages was now over.[1] The notion that such a place might really exist was replaced with philosophizing about

67

imagined, ideal societies, and with critical observations of one's own and others' vices and virtues by way of encomiums such as Erasmus's *Laus stultitiae* (In Praise of Folly), which he dedicated to Thomas More, and, for that matter, Montaigne's well-known essay on *les cannibales*.

I happen to be a fellow townsman of Erasmus Roterodamus, although the port city by the Maas of five hundred years ago had little in common with the modern one, especially since the Second World War. I was born just after that war in a town heavily scarred by bombing. Rotterdam's entire historic center, the original triangle within the city walls, was completely wiped out by German bombers in May 1940. Remarkably, the statue of Erasmus, the oldest public statue in the Netherlands, survived the conflagration unscathed, just as the humanistic message of this promoter of peace survived the terrible religious wars of the sixteenth century, and in fact the onslaught of the centuries, in his ironic adage: "Dulce bellum inexpertis" (War is sweet to those without experience of it).[2] It took several years to remove all the ruins, and close to my parents' home in the suburb of Kralingen, part of the rubble was dumped in a lake and turned into islands that now, fifty years later, idyllically covered with lawns, brush, and trees, look like a heavenly gift of nature. My whole youth was engulfed by the stamping and hissing sound of steam engines driving piles into the soft ground on which the new buildings of Rotterdam arose.

Unlike Nagasaki's citizens, who were bombed without warning five years later with a hundred times more destructive force, the vast majority of Rotterdam's burghers were able to flee the blaze when the German bombers attacked. The numbers are telling: in Nagasaki, almost 70,000 people died from the direct impact and another 75,000 from the aftereffects of the atom bomb, while in Rotterdam no more than 900 people were killed by the Stukas' incendiary bombs. In both cases, threats of more bombing of other cities brought an end to the hostilities: the Dutch were subjected to five years of German occupation and persecution; the Japanese to American occupation, but they were liberated from an oppressive militaristic regime.

Nowadays the carefully restored St. Laurens Church, dedicated to the tutelary saint of the sailors, with the statue of Erasmus in front of it, and Zadkine's dramatic sculpture *Town without Heart* overlooking the waterfront, remind us of Rotterdam's past. The Rotterdam of the 1950s and early 1960s in which I grew up was a bustling port city that in those years surpassed New York as the premier port in the world. The wide Maas River was chockablock with barges, tugboats, ferryboats, coasters, cargo liners, and tramp steamers, to say nothing of the stately passenger liners of the Holland-America Line, which docked in the middle of the city. All of that has vanished since the advent of intercontinental air traffic and container shipping, but it was an unforgettable sight that made virtually every adventurous boy dream of signing on to sail away over the horizon. Down by the docks one could find sailors roaming the quays, ship chandlers, boardinghouses, taverns, and, on the southern bank of the river, the red-light district of Katendrecht, which also happened to be the home of a sizable community of the so-called *Pinda Chinezen*, or "peanut Chinese."

In the 1950s port cities still had their own character, dynamic life, and romance, because the ships remained in the docks for a week or more, often close to or in the middle of town. Those who grew up in Boston when its wharves were still part of a working waterfront, not yuppie housing developments and marinas, will understand what I am talking about. Today travelers move around in planes, ports have been replaced by impersonal airport terminals, and the occasional visiting cruise liners look less like oceangoing vessels than floating toasters in a Disney film. That is not to say that ports do not exist anymore; like snakes shedding their skin, they have moved away from wharves near the city and closer to the sea, or in the case of Europort, today's version of Rotterdam, literally into the sea.

A closer look at the experience of living in a port city may help us explain the city's responses to its constantly changing environment. Rotterdam's ubiquitous *Pinda Chinezen* were as much an indication and reminder of historic change as the ruins of the city center. These men were among the thousands of Chinese sailors, mostly boilermen or stokers from the Wenzhou region in Zhejiang Province, who were laid off midvoyage during the Depression of the 1930s and now eked out a living selling peanut cookies in the street, crying, *"Pinda pinda lekka lekka!"* ("Peanut peanut tasty tasty!"). If ever there was a testimony to the effects of global trade on private life, it would seem to be the sorry tale of these peanut vendors.[3] But that is not the end of the story. When the postwar Dutch economy picked up again in the 1950s, the peanut Chinese disappeared one after another from the streets as they left to start their own Chinese restaurants. Within two decades these private enterprises mushroomed to such an extent that today there are more Chinese restaurants than any other kind of restaurant in the Netherlands.

Voices

This triptych of Batavia, Canton, and Nagasaki would not be complete if we did not meet with some of the individuals who made their living there and left us their recollections. Obviously it is impossible to devote equal space to all types of actors on the port-city scene. I must also confess that we are facing the problem of scarcity of sources. We may skip "exotic and peripheral groups" like the Iranun, who raided the coast of Sumatra and the Bangka Strait, and the Chinese pirates who knocked about Chinese coastal waters in the 1790s, if only because they did not actually descend on the ports of Batavia and Canton, although they certainly succeeded in destabilizing the traffic in the coastal waters.[4] But would it not be wonderful to hear Chinese *huashang* tell their tales? And what about female voices?

In the contemporary sources men occasionally refer to women, but we do not really hear the latter speak for themselves in the encounter between East and West, with that one remarkable exception, of course, of a formidable woman of Dutch-Japanese descent in Batavia, Cornelia van Nijenrode, who, notwithstanding the Japanese maritime prohibitions, continued to correspond with her mother in Japan.[5] A penny for the thoughts of the Tanka women who used to ferry foreigners in Canton and sometimes provided them with some extra care under the tarpaulin of their sampan's cabin, or the prostitutes of "Lob Lob Creek," "who," according to William Hickey, "if required so to do, board the boats passing up or down, and thus satisfy the carnal appetites of the people belonging to the ships, this being the only spot where opportunities of that nature offer."[6] Or what about the women who chose to share their lives with foreign husbands in Macao, like the Chinese wife of the Dutch supercargo Hemmingson. She followed him from Batavia to China, ran his household in Macao, and eventually accompanied him to the Netherlands, where they settled down in The Hague.[7] That possibility did not exist for the female companions of the Dutch on Deshima. Japanese *yujo*, "ladies of pleasure" from the famous Maruyama District in Nagasaki, were allowed to visit Deshima and cheer up the

Dutch ship entering Nagasaki harbor, early 1800s. Artist: Kawahara Keiga (1786–after 1860). Collection of Nagasaki Municipal Museum.

lonely Dutchmen confined on that little island, as the following *senryu* suggests: "*Maruyama no koi wa ichiman sanzenri*" ("Love at Maruyama bridges a distance of thirteen thousand miles").[8]

Female Voices

The only other distinct and articulate female voice that I have run across in the literature is that of the widow of the pirate chief Ching Yih, who became a chief herself and in the end acted as a voice of reason in persuading her followers to surrender en masse to the governor of Canton in 1811. The writer of the *Jinghai fenji* (History of the Pacification of the Pirates), which appeared in 1830, quotes her as saying to her followers when the game was up: "We being driven about on the ocean, without having any fixed habitation—pray let us go to Canton to inform the government, to state the reason of the recoiling waves, to clear up all doubts, and to agree on what day or in what place we shall make our submission." When her words did not produce the desired effect, she and some other women took the initiative to go to Canton to see the governor in person, forcing the pirates to admit that they were sending their wives to settle the surrender.[9]

One other female voice that has come to us is like Edvard Munch's compelling scream: it is the unstoppable shrieking and sobbing of a female slave, who was taken to Batavia by a Chinese merchant after he had purchased her on the island of Bali. During the sea voyage to Batavia the continuous wailing and shrieking of the girl so upset her new owner that he simply threw her overboard. It is but a glimpse of colonial life, but that shrieking woman will haunt those who read about her sad end in the Minutes of the Kong Koan of Batavia, that treasure trove of information on the daily life in an early modern Chinatown.[10]

Chinese Voices

Male Chinese voices expressing personal views about the encounters between East and West in these ports are rare. Even less do we hear from the Chinese merchant adventurers, the *huashang*, whose epic enterprise forms the warp and woof of these chapters. It would be absurd to suggest that the Chinese were so self-involved that they were not curious about foreigners or foreign cultures. It is well known that at a certain phase in his life, the Yongzheng Emperor himself (who reigned from 1722 to 1735) showed considerable interest in the architecture, manners, and dress of Europe. He has been portrayed wearing a periwig and dressed in Western clothes. The pavilions in the Yuan Ming Garden constructed by his successor, the Qianlong Emperor, reflected all kinds of Western architecture. Without doubt the Roman Catholic priests at the court had a hand in this.

Laura Hostetler has made the point that in the course of the eighteenth century, as the size of the Manchu empire almost doubled, the Manchus showed considerable "ethnographic" and "cartographic" interest in the people recently subjugated by them. She also notes the quest for knowledge about non-Chinese peoples on the empire's internal frontiers, which was carried out by official representatives of the Qing state with increasingly rigorous empirical methods.[11] Yet all of this interest seems to have added up to little more than pure description and depiction, rich in detail but lacking in depth. Even in Chinese novels of the period there is very little to be found about Sino-European interaction in Canton.

One of the very few Chinese who traveled overseas and left an account of his adventures in Java is Wang Dahai, who between 1783 and

1793 served as preceptor to the children of the Chinese captain of Pekalongan, a small port town on the north coast of Java. This learned Chinese sojourner did not have much patience with the indigenous people of the archipelago and wrote as little as possible about them. Considering that he actually lived on Java for ten years, the following description is no less than absurd: "Regarding the manners of the natives, with their uncouth forms, their singular appearances, dwelling in hollow trees, and residing in caverns, with their woolly hair and tattooed bodies, their naked persons and uncooked food, and all such monstrous and unheard of matters, it is scarcely worthwhile wasting one's breath upon them."[12]

The account Wang gives of Batavia and its European inhabitants is one of distance and Confucian condescension. He admired the buildings in the town but was very puzzled by the strange behavior of the Dutch: "Every seven days there is a religious ceremony when, from nine to eleven in the morning, they go to the place of worship, to recite prayers and mumble charms; the hearers hanging down their heads and weeping, as if there was something affecting in it all; but after half an hour's jabber they are allowed to disperse, and away they go to feast in their garden houses, and spend the whole day in delight, without attending to any business."[13]

Mr. Wang apparently did not feel comfortable in the barbarian regions. The feelings expressed about "otherness" or alienation abundantly show Wang Dahai's strong sense of his own identity as a *wen-ren*, a well-educated man, in eighteenth-century colonial Java. "There are no writings of philosophers and poets, wherewith to beguile the time; nor any friends of like mind, to soothe one's feelings; no deep caverns or lofty towers, to which one could resort for an excursion; all which is very much to be lamented."[14]

Home is where the heart is. For our present purposes it is interesting to note a rhapsody by Luo Fangbo, the founding father of the Lanfang *kongsi* (clan association) on Kalimantan. Luo Fangbo pours out his heart about his sojourn in the gold-mining regions of West Borneo. A few lines from this poem clearly evoke his "out of place" feeling:

> Now this place lies in the tropical zone
> The sun fills the air with humid, steaming vapours
> The vegetation really knows no season here . . .

> Things are called by different names
> and the Chinese and the barbarians speak entirely different
>   tongues . . .
> Alas! In this barbarian dwelling under torrential rains,
> My body wastes away under heavy toils . . .
> Among this great scenery of mountains and waters,
> I cannot but weep at all these wasted years![15]

Could it be that the Chinese abroad simply were filled with homesickness? One thing is certain: we find a startling lack of interest in Western affairs on the part of the Chinese. Occasionally one runs across a sentimental poem about a Western object such as a rusty sword, a *jiaban quan* (a Western square-rigger) with rigging like cobwebs, or curious stories in contemporary novels about strange Western contraptions used for erotic purposes. There actually is a Chinese novel about the foreign trade in Canton: the *Shenlouzi* by Yushan Laozi, which was published in 1804. Unfortunately, not one word is wasted on the foreign devils themselves, although the author shows great interest in Western curiosa, such as the 28 clocks, 182 large and small watches, and mirrors and glassware that were seized from a corrupt and abusive *Hoppo* (the customs official), and also automatons that served wine and two very ingenious foreign-made beds designed for deflowering young virgins.[16] It is a bit disappointing, but there it is.

Japanese Voices

In marked contrast to the lack of interest in foreigners among the Chinese, we find quite a number of narratives by the Japanese about fleeting encounters with Dutchmen or with Western objects and inventions. More important, these accounts make it possible for us to gauge how the writers responded to Western ideas and to follow them in their attempts to translate Western medical and scientific works and make them accessible to their fellow Japanese. What is most apparent from the surviving Chinese and Japanese literature is that while an author like Wang Dahai seems to have been interested mainly in disparaging the customs and manners of the barbarians, a select group of Japanese scholars and artists called *rangakusha* (students of Dutch learning), or *rampeki* (those "hooked" on Holland), reveal, as Donald

Keene has put it, "extreme inquisitiveness mixed with the fondness for the exotic," and also a new restless and receptive spirit that was herding the Japanese public into a new age—that of modern Japan.[17] There is no way in which I can do justice here to these Japanese scholars of the late eighteenth century, but fortunately Timon Screech, Martha Chaiklin, Calvin French, and many others have published widely on the innovative techniques that sprang from Japan's encounter with the West.[18]

That this receptive mood would emerge in the relatively isolated island empire of Japan is surprising. In spite of the maritime prohibitions, or *kaikin*, Japanese sailors who had been blown off course or shipwrecked occasionally washed up on far-away foreign shores. In the rare cases when these castaways made it back home, they were thoroughly debriefed by the shogunal authorities, who normally went to great lengths to keep them from telling others what they had seen and experienced abroad. Probably the best-known peregrinations are those of Kodayu, a Japanese ship captain from Ise, who, after seven months of drifting in the Pacific in 1783, washed up in the Aleutian Islands, which were then Russian territory. He and his surviving shipmates ended up several years later in Kamchatka and from there were taken to Irkutsk in Siberia. In Irkutsk he met with a Finnish scholar, Erik Laxman, who took the Japanese survivors to St. Petersburg, where they were granted an audience with Catherine the Great.[19]

In 1792 Kodayu and two remaining companions were escorted back to the port of Nemuro on Ezo (Hokkaido) in northern Japan by Laxman's son, who also delivered a letter from the Russian government asking for trading privileges. The curt but polite answer that Laxman took home was that he had come to the wrong address and that a request for trade should be made at Nagasaki, the usual place for all dealings with foreigners. Not until 1804 did the Russians send an envoy, Count Resanov, to Nagasaki. After Kodayu had been debriefed by the shogunal authorities, the physician and *rangakusha* Katsuragawa Hoshu took it upon himself to interrogate the former castaway in more detail about his experiences. His notes were published as *Hokusa bunryaku* (A Brief Report on the Castaways in the North) and included a short description of Russia, drawn from a Dutch book that had been given to Hoshu by Gijsbert Hemmij, the Dutch factory head on Deshima.[20]

The interior of the chief factor's room at Deshima, 1794. Artist: Shiba Kokan.
Shiba Kōkan, *Nagasaki e kikō: saiyū ryodan* (Edo, Nagasaki, Illustrated Account of a
Western Journey). Collection of the author.

The miraculous adventures of Kodayu were not taken seriously by
all Japanese. One reader, Shiba Kokan, a Japanese painter, bon vivant,
and *rangakusha* of sorts, was very critical of the book. Kokan loved to
experiment with Western art techniques. Using a Dutch drawing manual, he had taught himself perspective and shading; he prided himself
on having made the first copper etchings in Japan; and he prepared his
own colored oil pigments for his Western-style paintings. If his experi-
ments in oil painting cannot be compared with the fine craftsmanship
of Chinese painters at Canton, who had quickly learned how to imitate
Western art, Kokan did express his ideas clearly in an essay on Western
art, writing that Western painting represented a more profound way of
looking at nature than did the traditional Chinese and Japanese way of
using the brush.[21]

Curious to see the Dutch in their lodgings on Deshima, Kokan made
the long trip to Nagasaki in 1788, which he described in his *Kōkan saiyū
nikki* (Diary of Kokan's Trip to the West).[22] He made many drawings
on the way, and at Hirado he drew a picture of the small pagoda erected
in honor of that local paragon of filial piety, Cornelia van Nijenrode,

the banished daughter of a Dutch merchant and his Japanese wife, who continued to send secret letters to her mother from Batavia.[23] On Deshima, Kokan made a quick sketch of the room of the factory chief, who, knowing very well that this was a rather exotic interior to Japanese eyes and seeing that his Japanese visitor was looking at all the paintings on the wall, asked him if he liked it. Kokan, although he felt a bit slighted by this condescending question, replied "that he was dazzled by the splendor."[24] With his curiosity for everything strange, Kokan forms in fact the ideal *trait d'union* between Japan and the West.

Now that we have seen some Chinese and Japanese impressions of visitors from the West, I would like to turn to three Dutch individuals. Andreas van Braam Houckgeest, Isaac Titsingh, and Hendrik Doeff lived and worked in East and Southeast Asia in the period under study. What they all have in common is that they have been described by their contemporaries as block-headed *"Mynheeren"* who stood in the way of early nineteenth-century progress, or by esteemed scholars such as Donald Keene as "willing to submit to [such] indignities [as kowtowing] in the hope of profit . . . most of them completely uninterested in Japan."[25] Such epithets reflect the typical bias of contemporary Englishmen, who believed the world was waiting to be enlightened by them, and also the view of the occasional Orientalist today who measures Westerners of the past by his own social background and education, without really knowing much about the worldview, background, or education of these Dutchmen, or even the circumstances in which they lived and worked.

In one way or another, these three gentlemen—Van Braam, Titsingh, and Doeff—shed light on the period that concerns us here. Their importance derives not as much from the decisive roles they played at the time (although for nationalist reasons, Doeff turned out to be a celebrated figure in his day) as from the fact that they were on the spot at a moment when everything seemed to be in flow, and have left us vivid eyewitness accounts of the final days of the Dutch East India Company and the chaotic times in which they lived.

It so happens that all three men have recently been saved from relative obscurity. A few years ago a biography of Titsingh was published in Dutch by Frank Lequin, and a slightly hurried study by Timon Screech appeared in 2006.[26] The revival of interest in A. E. van Braam Houckgeest and Hendrik Doeff is due to the efforts of their North

American descendants. In the early 1990s Edward Barnsley of New-town, Pennsylvania, published an exhaustive biography about his mer-curial ancestor Van Braam, and Hendrik Doeff's *Herinneringen van Japan* (Recollections of Japan) was translated from the original Dutch by Annick Doeff.[27]

Isaac Titsingh

Isaac Titsingh (1745–1812) was the scion of a distinguished burgher family of physicians with close ties to the VOC management in Am-sterdam. What made him unusual as a Company servant was his excel-lent education. He joined the physicians' guild of Amsterdam in 1764 and one year later he obtained a doctorate in law at Leiden University. During his years in the service of the VOC, Titsingh served in Batavia, Japan, and India, and finally headed an embassy to the Qianlong Em-peror of China. During the forty-four months that Titsingh intermit-tently spent in Japan in between 1779 and 1784, he developed a pro-found interest in things Japanese, and he tried to learn as much as possible about the country and its people from his isolated position on Deshima. Under difficult circumstances he gained the confidence of one of the governors of Nagasaki and of Lord Shimazu, the daimyo of Satsuma, who actually became the father-in-law of the shogun. Unlike any Dutchman before him, Titsingh developed personal friendships with some of these people in high positions.

It was Titsingh's intention to devote himself fully to the study of Ja-pan after his retirement and to oversee the publication of Japanese sources in English and French translations. To put it in his own words, "It was his ambition to gain more knowledge of a nation so civilized, so inquisitive, and so little estimated at its true value in Europe."[28] Even after he left Japan and became director of the VOC factory at Chinsura in Bengal, he continued to correspond with his friends in Japan about matters of Japanese history, and he also enlisted the help of his succes-sors at Deshima. All these correspondents contributed in one way or another to the collection of materials for his magnum opus. It was no easy matter for Titsingh to keep this correspondence going. On one occasion a VOC ship, the *Belvliet*, sank near Burma, taking with it batches of carefully copied and edited materials.[29] It is from Titsingh's intimate correspondence with one of his successors in particular, Van Reede, that we get a closer insight into his personal fancies and also the loves he could not forget, such as his female companion Oekinisan, who was now at Van Reede's side. As the latter wrote him: "Oekinisan is sitting right now next to me on the *canapé* [sofa] playing the samisen, which is her usual amusement and occupation while I am working, and to which I have grown so accustomed, that her music doesn't disturb me the least."[30] Even though she was well taken care of, Titsingh continued to send his former Japanese mistress little presents, such as a ring and calico fabrics.

Upon his departure on his second trip to Japan, at the end of June 1781, Titsingh was already aware of black clouds massing on the horizon. On 12 June 1781 the governor-general and councilors in Batavia had received the (unofficial) news that England had declared war on the Dutch Republic in December 1780. Immediately they sent letters to all their offices in the East to inform their representatives of this disaster and to warn them against any English attempts to take possession of Dutch settlements. Titsingh carried this letter with him to Japan, conscious of the fact that if war really had been declared, Batavia might be unable to send a ship to Japan in the following year.

When no Dutch ship appeared on the roadstead of Deshima because of the Anglo-Dutch War, Titsingh chose not to disclose the real reason to the Japanese. Instead, he used this opportunity to vent his feelings about the impolite treatment he and his men often received at Deshima. He told the governor of Nagasaki that this probably was the reason why no ship had been sent: the Batavian government was tired of the Japanese authorities' high-handed treatment of its servants. Titsingh apparently spent some of his leisure time reading the factory archives in Deshima, and he dug up a letter written in 1641(!) by Governor-General Antonio van Diemen to the *opperhoofd* of Deshima, Johan van Elseracq, in which the latter was advised "that we [the Dutch] do not come to Japan to serve her, and to obey her strict laws, but to enjoy the profits from the trade."[31] On this occasion the governor of Nagasaki, who clearly was concerned about the nonarrival of the annual Dutch ship, asked Titsingh for the building plans for an East Indiaman so that the Japanese could build a Dutch ship themselves, which would be used for the transport of copper from Osaka to Nagasaki. Titsingh took him at his word and provided him instead with information on how to build a Dutch sailing barge of the type used to transport cargoes in the coastal waters of Holland.[32]

Five years later his successor, Hendrik Romberg, saw the ship that had been constructed on the basis of the information provided by Titsingh and some Chinese shipwrights, who had also been consulted:

> The interpreters came to tell me that a barge, which had been made after the ship model of a barge which was sent here three years ago, has arrived from Osaka. It can hold roughly twice as much as an ordinary large barge . . . The Japanese call it *sankoekmal*—which means "copied from three countries," namely Holland, China and Japan—but it does not resemble anything either Dutch or Chinese, and glancing at it, it does not seem possible that it can carry that much cargo, but I am used to the fact that the Japanese are prone to exaggeration.[33]

A few months later Romberg was informed that the "three-countries ship" had run aground on its way to Matsumae in northern Japan. The Dutch chief of Deshima almost triumphantly concluded: "Thus it is proved that they [the Japanese] should not busy themselves trying to copy something strange, for they do not know how to handle it, as I myself witnessed, when it came sailing into the bay." The first Japanese attempts to design a hybrid vessel within the limitations of the existing *kaikin* regulations thus misfired.[34]

Many, many years later, in 1859, a Dutch naval commander visited a port in southern Kyushu and to his surprise saw what looked like a very antique ghost ship. When he asked after the origins of this curious three-master with its red lacquered hull, he was told that it had been built along the lines of a Dutch East Indiaman as recently as 1852 at Mito, just one year before Commodore Perry arrived at Shimoda Bay. Clearly the dream of building a real sailing ship along the lines of a VOC ship had continued to haunt the Japanese shipwrights, yet when they at last built one, they were at least a century late.[35]

Here we briefly take leave of Titsingh, but we will meet him again soon in his last commission in the service of the Dutch East India Company, as envoy to the Qianlong Emperor, a rather arduous mission

Andreas Everardus van Braam Houckgeest (1739–1801), in 1795. Anonymous Chinese painter. Collection of Stichting van Braam Houckgeest.

that he carried out in the company of the person to whom I would now like to turn.

Andreas Everardus van Braam Houckgeest

If there ever was anybody who resembled Voltaire's Candide in real life, it was Andreas Everardus van Braam Houckgeest (1739–1801), better known in America as Van Braam. Notwithstanding the ups and downs in his eventful life, he always saw "le meilleur des choses dans ce meilleur des mondes," the best of all possible worlds. It is easy to poke fun at this larger-than-life, rotund character, who had a mercurial temper. As his American grandson Cincinnatus Roberts later recollected, after giving vent to one of his not infrequent fits of thundering anger, Van Braam could be overheard plucking his guitar, softly singing, a fado perhaps, in a falsetto voice.[36] Van Braam was a very interesting man—a polyglot, a declared supporter of the American Revolution and the enlightened ideas of the patriot movement in the Netherlands, a writer of tracts and manuals (including a Portuguese grammar), a lover of women, a man who actually carried out his ideas, and who twice tried to build a new life in the United States. All this can be best summarized in his personal motto, *In magnis Voluisse sat est* (In matters of great importance, striving is enough), which, incidentally, was also used by Erasmus in his *In Praise of Folly*.

Van Braam received his early training as a cadet in the Dutch navy. Independent and adventurous by nature, he decided to leave the service at the age of nineteen and signed up with the VOC on one of the Company's first direct voyages to Canton. On his second trip home from China, in 1763, he made a stop at the Cape of Good Hope to marry Catharina Cornelia Gertruida, Baroness Van Reede van Oudtshoorn, the third daughter (among thirteen children) of the local Dutch governor. After one more long stint at Canton, Van Braam decided in 1773 that he had amassed a large enough fortune to repatriate and live with his family as a person of independent means. Back in Holland he soon got interested in local politics and became a promoter of the Enlightenment-inspired democratic patriot movement. He followed with no less enthusiasm the developments in America when the Revolution broke out, even writing letters of recommendation to Benjamin Franklin on behalf of his cousins who wished to join the American navy. This particular moment in Dutch history and its direct links with the early history of the United States of America have been well documented by two eminent American historians: Simon Schama, in his *Patriots and Liberators*, and Barbara Tuchman, in *The First Salute*.[37] The latter title refers to the first salute given to the Stars and Stripes, on 16 November 1776, by the Dutch governor of the Caribbean island of St. Eustatius, which acted as a main supply station for the Americans in the early years of the Revolution. This and other behavior by the Dutch, who chose to stay neutral, was the final straw for the British. They were certainly aware of the considerable financial help given by the Dutch Republic to the Americans. In December 1780 the British declared war against the Dutch, and a little more than a month later Admiral Rodney carried out a hatchet job on St. Eustatius, the "Golden Rock," from which it would not recover until cruise-ship tourism put it back on the map in the last decades of the twentieth century.[38]

When the Fourth Anglo-Dutch War broke out, trade came to a complete stop. Because the patriot movement failed to make much headway in Dutch politics, Van Braam impetuously sold all his belongings and in 1783 took his wife and five children to the United States, where he settled in Charleston, South Carolina, as a merchant and rice farmer. In the spring of 1784 he acquired American citizenship. The family's emigration turned into a colossal personal tragedy, however. Shortly after the Van Braams had established themselves in Charleston four of the children died in a diphtheria epidemic, and not long afterward the paterfamilias was duped out of his money by his new business associates—or perhaps his own business deals, "always conducted by devious means and involved transactions," had proved his undoing.[39]

Heartbroken, Van Braam was forced to return to the Netherlands with his wife, but they left behind their first daughter, who had married an American gentleman, Captain Richard Brooke Roberts, the forefather of the family historian Edward Barnsley. Back in Holland, Van Braam was able to sign up once more for the position of supercargo in Canton. Thus we find him back in China in July 1790, where he immediately began to rebuild his personal wealth, now with the help of American shipping. Thanks to Barnsley's research we know that, as a sideline to his VOC duties, Van Braam bought or loaded at least seven American ships for private trade during the years 1792 to 1795.[40] Even Amasa Delano, the famous Yankee adventurer, was involved in affairs with Van Braam, but having lost a great sum of money he chose to remain remarkably taciturn about those ventures in his travel account.[41] How risky affairs of trade were we learn from the correspondence of Charles de Constant, a Swiss merchant in French service, who left an incisive eyewitness account of the trade at Canton.[42] Jean Baptiste Piron wrote De Constant, who had returned to Geneva: "Van Braam is a terrific fellow for business, this is the third vessel freighted by him for Ostende [in Belgium]. He sends a fourth, freighted with tea, to New York as soon as an American shows up. Then the cargo is bought by him, and sent away with unbelievable speed. I am afraid that he will have to suffer for it; these vessels all are in bad condition and will have to pass the Cape of Good Hope in the bad season."[43]

As head of the Canton factory, Van Braam noted with particular glee the failure of the Macartney embassy to the court of the Qianlong Emperor in 1793. It was well known to the European merchants in Canton that the British aspired to secure a foothold of their own in the Canton delta, and this plan now fell through. (It would not be achieved until the seizure of Hong Kong with the Nanjing Treaty in 1842.)

In an act of one-upmanship, Van Braam devised a plan of his own that would enable him to travel through China, see the country, and describe it in a travelogue as his Dutch predecessors had done twice in the seventeenth century. Both of those journeys had resulted in well-known illustrated works that had been translated into many languages. He wrote a letter to the governor-general in Batavia stating that the viceroy of Canton had invited all Western trading nations to send an envoy to the Qianlong Emperor to congratulate him on the sixtieth anniversary of his reign. And although all the other nations failed to follow up on this invitation, the government of Batavia decided to delegate Isaac Titsingh, who had just returned from Chinsura, to head its embassy to the Manchu throne. Titsingh had actually entertained the British envoy Macartney when he visited Batavia on his way to China in the spring of 1793.[44]

A lot of ink has been spent on the embassy of Lord Macartney to the Qing court, by Macartney himself; by his second-in-command, Staunton; by the secretary to the mission, Barrow; and by a footman, Anderson, who accompanied him. Anderson was the first to write about the diplomatic failure, immortalizing it with the words: "We entered Peking like paupers; we remained in it like prisoners; and we quitted it like vagrants."[45] Later historians of trade, such as Morse, Pritchard, Greenberg, and Dermigny, also wrote about this embassy.[46]

But the best known work on the topic is by the French politician Alain Peyrefitte, who, on the occasion of the embassy's two-hundredth anniversary, wrote an entertaining book on the failed enterprise.[47] Entertaining because it is well written and well researched, but also because of the light it throws on Peyrefitte himself. For those who have read his writings on China over the years, books with such prophetic titles as *Quand la Chine s'éveillera* (When China Awakes), *Un choc de cultures* (A Shock of Cultures), and *La Chine s'éveille* (China Awakes), it is clear that Peyrefitte's underlying theme has been the simple mantra: If only Chairman Mao had listened to me when I met him as President De Gaulle's special envoy in 1969!

Yet what an academic enterprise Peyrefitte undertook. He sagaciously hired a team of sinologists to translate documents from the Chinese archives. Like so many authors before and even after him, he had a hang-up about the kowtow ritual, even implying that Macartney did kowtow when nobody was looking.[48] In the wake of Peyrefitte's book and the inevitable commemorations of the Macartney bicentennial, there followed a wave of critical writings that I shall not go into here because it would take us too far away from our subject.[49] Suffice it to say that a lot of attention has been paid to such fashionable issues as the "meaning of ritual" and cross-cultural understanding.[50] It is curious how the fuss that was made in the nineteenth century about the kowtow as a sign of Manchu arrogance continues to occupy the mind.

Much nonsense has been written about the supposedly humiliating aspects of the Titsingh and Van Braam mission, not only in their own time but also recently, although a very enlightening early article about their undertaking was written by J. J. L. Duyvendak in 1938.[51] Without doubt the hasty trip made by Titsingh and Van Braam and their party to Peking in the winter of 1794 was a very strenuous enterprise for the middle-aged envoys and not at all what they had imagined an embassy to the Chinese emperor to be like. As Titsingh wrote in his account, he was shocked that he had to leave Canton immediately: "This news I found very disagreeable, because of the inconveniences of cold and discomfort to which one is exposed in such a severe and raw season, and which urgently required the necessary provision, and because of the fatigues of the journey which then for the greater part, the rivers being frozen, would have to be continued overland."[52]

Haste was suddenly required because the Qianlong Emperor was so enthusiastic when he heard about the Dutch intentions in the autumn. He issued a decree to the ministers of the Grand Council, writing, "This will be a splendid event!" and decided that the well-wishers should not postpone their journey to the capital until the next spring but should leave Canton immediately so that they could congratulate him "one or two days prior to the twentieth day of the twelfth month, the day on which we close the seals, in order that they, together with the princes and dukes of Mongolia and the ambassadors from various

The reception of the Dutch envoys at Canton, 1794. Artist unknown. A. E. van
Braam Houckgeest, *Voyage de l'ambassade de la Compagnie des Indes Orientales
hollandaises, vers l'empereur de la Chine, dans les années 1794 & 1795 . . .*
(Philadelphia, 1797–1798).

countries of the outer frontier may be regaled with banquets and presents." The emperor noted that the Dutch memorial was written under
the names of the great ministers of the East India Company, Ni Debo
(Nederburgh) and other officials, acting for their king. When some
members in his cabinet wondered whether this did not deviate from
the established regulations, the Son of Heaven remarked: "What need
is there to go so deeply into the matter? Of course, We should approve
their coming to Peking and presenting themselves at an audience in order to justify their sincerity in turning toward Our civilization and ad-
miring Our justice."[53]

Given all the theorizing scholars recently have engaged in, it is refreshing to see from this decree to what extent ritual considerations
played a predominant role. When his ministers pointed out that the
Dutch envoys were sent not directly by their "king" but by the Dutch
East India Company, the emperor did not mind at all, so long as they
behaved themselves properly. Their presence could only heighten the
festivities.

On 20 January 1795, Chinese New Year's Day, the VOC ambassadors were received, together with the ambassadors of Korea, at the

Baohe Palace, where they were presented with wine upon having performed the customary kowtows. In the days that followed, Van Braam and Titsingh were invited to visit the imperial gardens, where they actually toasted the emperor and even went skating, to their own amusement and that of the imperial ménage. Afterward, in contrast to the rigors of their trip to the capital, the return from Peking to Canton in the early spring was a very pleasant affair during which they had plenty of time to visit places of interest.

Here are two quotes from critics who were ignorant of the diplomatic conduct of VOC officials in Asia. The first comes from John Barrow, who participated in the Macartney mission. Barrow was a personal friend of Titsingh, who would not have appreciated the way Barrow portrayed him in his *Travels in China*, published in 1805. According to Barrow, the two Dutch ambassadors "cheerfully submitted to every humiliating ceremony required from them by the Chinese, who, in return, treated them in the most contemptuous and indignant manner."[54] The American missionary and China watcher Samuel Wells Williams, the author of that celebrated work on China, *The Middle Kingdom*, plagiarized Aeneas Anderson when he wrote in 1848: "They were brought to the capital like malefactors, treated when there like beggars, and then sent back to Canton like mountebanks, to perform the three times three prostration at all times and before everything their conductors saw fit. Van Braam's own account of his embassy is one of the most humiliating records of ill-requited obsequiousness before insolent government lackeys which any European was ever called upon to pen."[55] Could it be that Williams became so enraged by the ritual because he knew that Van Braam was actually an American national?

Delegated as envoys of the Dutch East India Company to congratulate the emperor, and not as ambassadors of a king or a czar, Van Braam and Titsingh saw no reason to trouble themselves about kowtowing or behaving in China as the Chinese did. They actually reaffirmed this to the viceroy in Canton, telling him that "they were quite willing to follow the customs of the country they were visiting, even more so if it concerned the emperor whom they came to congratulate on his long reign."[56] For Titsingh, who had twice visited the shogun in Edo, where an audience required all kinds of ceremonial kowtowing on the tatami of the shogunal palace, all this was much ado about nothing.

Titsingh and Van Braam lived worlds apart from the prevailing West-

ern mindset in the nineteenth century. Witness a paper that former
U.S. president John Quincy Adams read to the Massachusetts Historical Society in 1840 in defense of the recent English intervention at
Canton. According to Adams, opium was no more the cause of the outbreak of hostilities than the throwing of the tea into Boston Harbor
had been the cause of the Revolutionary War in America. "The cause
of the war is the *kowtow*—the arrogant and insupportable pretensions
of China, that she will hold commercial intercourse with the rest of
mankind, not upon terms of equal reciprocity, but upon the insulting
and degrading forms of relations between lord and vassal."[57]

Upon their return to Canton, the paths of Titsingh and Van Braam
parted when they heard that French troops had invaded the Netherlands. Rather than return home, Titsingh embarked on an English vessel, taking his large collection of manuscripts and Japonalia to England,
where he remained until the Treaty of Amiens in 1803 made it possible
for him to visit his family in Amsterdam. When war broke out again he
decided to remain on the Continent, and thenceforth he summered
in Amsterdam and wintered in Paris, where he sought out the com-
panionship of fellow Orientalists, who would eventually take care of
Titsingh's writings and publish part of them posthumously under the
title *Mémoires et anecdotes sur la dynastie régnante des djogouns.*[58]

Van Braam's further adventures were more eventful. While in Canton, he ordered a China service for the wife of the American president,
Martha Washington, and a complete suite of furniture for a new house
he was planning to build for himself in the United States. He then
leased a ship and set out for Philadelphia. En route, he called at the
Cape Colony (South Africa), where he took on board a nineteen-year-
old orphaned cousin of his estranged wife, with the promise that he
would take care of her education—although this may have been in a
more intimate way than her family members on the Cape had expected.

After his arrival in Philadelphia, Van Braam fraternized in that city
with famous French *evacués* like Talleyrand and Moreau de Saint-Méry.
With the help of Moreau he published a beautifully illustrated account
of his experience in China titled *Voyage de l'ambassade de la Compagnie
des Indes Orientales hollandaises, vers l'empereur de la Chine, dans les années
1794 & 1795 en deux tomes* (Voyage of the Embassy of the Dutch East
India Company to the Emperor of China in the Years 1794 and 1795,
in Two Volumes). He spent, and lost, a fortune on his masterpiece.

A curious fate befell this work after its publication, on account of which it was later grossly misinterpreted: 500 copies of the first of the two volumes printed in Philadelphia were sent to Europe to be sold there but were intercepted by a French privateer. This first volume was subsequently printed in two volumes by a French publisher, who declared it to be the complete narrative, before the second Philadelphia volume had even appeared. The pirated two-volume edition published in France in 1798 was subsequently translated into English (1798), German (1798–1799), and Dutch (1804–1806) editions, all of which included only the text of the first volume of Van Braam's work, a fact that has often been ignored. And—to keep the story brief—this circumstance may explain the bad press that the Dutch embassy has been given by later readers.

The first volume includes a dedication to George Washington, an *avertissement* (preface) by Moreau, and the text of Van Braam's journal up to 4 April 1795. This covers the quick winter voyage the well-wishers had to make to reach the emperor in time for the festivities in Peking. Reading the pirated edition—the edition we find in nearly all American libraries, including the Houghton Library at Harvard—one gets the impression that the Dutch simply hurried along, without seeing anything or staying in pleasant places. Because the account in the pirated edition stops somewhere in the middle of China, it was generally believed that this had been such a strenuous and uninteresting trip that the author had wisely stopped writing after he had begun his return journey to Canton.

The second volume of the original American edition was published in 1798. It includes the remainder of the original text of Van Braam's journal up to September 1796, and as it turns out, the envoys enjoyed a very comfortable and leisurely trip back to Canton, during which they were feted wherever they went.[59]

During his time in Philadelphia, Van Braam also devoted much of his attention to the construction of his *"chateau en Amerique,"* a colossal mansion he called China's Retreat, on the banks of the Delaware River. He greatly overspent on the house, which was a marvel of conspicuous consumption, and he had to sell it shortly after he moved in—but not before he married his Cape bride, who was forty years his junior. Once more thoroughly discouraged by his American misfortunes, which this time also amounted to a loss of face, Van Braam finally decided to return with his young wife to the Netherlands. He died there, after a few more peregrinations through Germany, in 1801.

One final note on Van Braam: For many years he was mainly remembered because of the China service he had offered to Martha Washington, plates decorated with a garland design depicting the names of the American states in a curious orthography, and a motto that has led many a person astray. It reads "DECUS ET TUTAMEN AB ILLO," which has been lamely translated as "Glory and Arms from That." The first three words should not offer any problem; they are actually the legend incused on the British pound piece, generally translated as "Ornament and Safeguard," which is somewhat different from the quotation "Decus et tutamen in armis" from Virgil's *Aeneid* (book 5, line 262), which means "Glory and honor in arms." Without doubt the correct reading of the legend on the China should be "Glory and Honor *Away from* Him," referring to the secession of the American states from the English king's control, showing once more the kind of joke Van Braam liked to play on his former neighbors in Canton.[60]

A Meeting of the Minds

While Titsingh and Van Braam were hurrying to Peking, a memorable meeting took place in Edo, the shogunal capital of Japan, on 1 January 1795. At the Shirando Academy, the famous *rangakusha* Otsuki Gentaku (1757–1827), translator of the *Heelkundige onderwijzingen*, or Textbook of Medicine, by Lorens Heister (1683–1758), gave a New Year's party in Dutch style in honor of the shipwrecked Captain Kodayu, who had finally returned to Japan two years before. Such New Year's parties had been the norm on Deshima, where every year the Dutch factory head regaled the entire corps of interpreters with Dutch food and drink to celebrate the solar New Year. This particular meeting of *rangakusha* has been immortalized by one of the participants, the painter Ichikawa Gakuzan. Thanks to an explanatory study by Reinier Hesselink of the many hidden meanings in this *peinture à clef*, it is now known who was present at that gathering of some of the most prominent Japanese students of Dutch learning and culture.[61]

Kodayu is depicted in the center as the guest of honor, next to the host. On the wall we see a portrait of Dr. Heister, whose work Otsuki Gentaku had translated. On the left we see the painter Shiba Kokan,

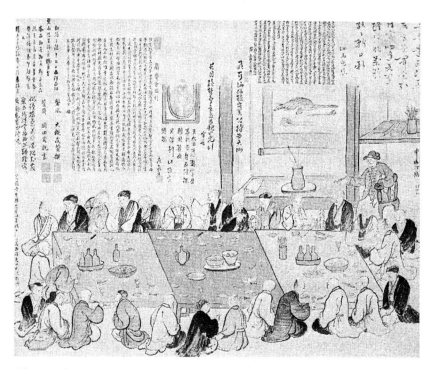

The Dutch New Year's Eve party at the Shirando Academy, 1795. Artist: Ichikawa Gakuzan. Collection of Waseda University Library.

whom we met early in this chapter. Shiba had actually questioned the truth of Kodayu's tales, but he himself was not taken very seriously by his fellow *rangakusha*, who thought him lacking in profundity and, in short, "a dilettante who thought highly of himself and went round bragging to people."[62]

The ensemble depicted in the painting includes some individuals who had been close friends of Titsingh's during his stay in Japan, and some who would become friends of Hendrik Doeff, the last person I would like to introduce.

Hendrik Doeff

In many respects a representative of a younger generation and a new age, Hendrik Doeff (1777–1835) arrived on Deshima in 1799 to serve as a scribe. He found the island in complete disarray. Gijsbert Hemmij, the factory head, had died during the court journey to the shogun;

most of Nagasaki and part of Deshima had been reduced to ashes in a conflagration; and the American ship *Eliza* had foundered near the entrance to the bay. Finding the accounts in utter disorder and beyond his ability to reorganize, Doeff returned to Batavia on the ship on which he had come. The next year he and the newly appointed factory head, Willem Wardenaar, returned to Nagasaki on the American ship the *Massachusetts*. Working together in the years that followed, the two of them were able to restore everything to order. When Wardenaar went home in 1803, he transferred his responsibilities on Deshima to Doeff. No Dutch VOC ships had reached the island since 1795, but every year one or two ships from neutral nations such as Denmark, Brandenburg, and the United States, were chartered to serve the Batavia trade with Japan. Most of them sailed under the Stars and Stripes, but when the Japanese shore came in sight that flag would be lowered and the Dutch tricolor hoisted, to play according to the Japanese rules, which allowed only ships from the Netherlands to enter Nagasaki Bay.[63]

Between 1797 and 1807, the year of President Jefferson's embargo, eleven American ships called at Deshima.[64] Many of the logbooks and cargo lists of these ships have been preserved in archives in New England, but to my knowledge, only one eyewitness account of the time has so far been published in full. This is the diary of William Cleveland, captain's clerk on board the *Massachusetts*, the ship that brought Doeff and Wardenaar to Japan in the summer of 1800.[65] Kanai Madoka, the editor of the text, added to it detailed information about the conditions under which the ship acquired its cargo in Batavia and the bill of lading.

The *Massachusetts* sailed from Java to Japan in thirty days—a swift passage—and arrived at the Nagasaki roadstead on 16 July. Captain Hutchings and his Dutch passengers moved to Deshima, but William Cleveland had to stay on board and was allowed ashore only five times during the ship's four-month stay. He spent most of the time on deck, taking care of the loading and unloading of the ship or gazing at traffic in the bay and the city in the background, contemplating Japan and things Japanese and noting down what others told him about the suppression of the Christian religion in Japan and the curious form of government in the Japanese empire.

Cleveland was perplexed by the careful body search to which those who went ashore were subjected, and supposed that Wardenaar "was renouncing the Christian religion" when he saw him paying his respects to a Japanese official, but "was afterwards assured that it was only a compliment" (in the Japanese manner). He was astonished to find out that the Japanese had a very low regard for America, but was quick to point out to them with the aid of a map how many times bigger it was than Holland. He heard about the severe maritime prohibitions forbidding the Japanese from going overseas and he even referred to Kodayu and his shipmates (without mentioning their names), who, after their return from Russia, "were confined and not permitted to see even their wives and children."

On the evening of 1 September, he witnessed an "innumerable number of lights, which appeared like Gold" on the surrounding mountains as the townspeople set up lanterns at the burial grounds on the occasion of Urabon, the Feast of the Souls. A few days later, when he was told about "public licensed brothels" in Nagasaki and how parents were selling into prostitution their three-, four-, and five-year-old daughters for two or three dollars, he could not "but pity the misfortunes of the Japan females & think with Affection of our own Country, & of the fond sisters of America who are so necessary to our happiness."[66] On 29 September, the governor of Nagasaki and a large retinue visited a Chinese junk anchored nearby and then came aboard the *Massachusetts*. After the Japanese governor had been wined and dined and shown around, Cleveland wrote, "He expressed a wish to see Peter Guss, our Cook, who is a very large Black man, who was ordered on deck; the Governor was pleased, probably he never saw an African before. After he had satisfied his curiosity he went into the Boat & as she shoo'd off we gave him three cheer's, which pleased the Japanders very much."[67] This account was indeed an impression of Japan as seen from the deck of a ship at anchor in a harbor, but it is probably quite representative of the views of a discerning sailor at the time.

Of the American captains who called at Nagasaki, Hendrik Doeff would later write, all were sincere and gentlemanly with the exception of two, who were drunkards. How serious and well prepared the captains were for their job can be judged from the ships' papers preserved today. So detailed are they that it is still possible to track down various objects listed in them in the collection of the Peabody Essex Museum in Salem.

Isaac Titsingh himself received a visit in London from an American ship captain named Henry Lelar, "a very accomplished gentleman speaking the most important languages of Europe," who came to ask him for advice about the private merchandise he should carry to Japan on his imminent voyage. Titsingh, who saw this as an opportunity to consign some letters to his Japanese friends, gladly complied.[68]

I shall not go into further detail here about the Americans on Deshima, but I should mention several other visits by foreign nationals to Nagasaki in which Hendrik Doeff came to play an important role. The first was the arrival in 1804 of the Russian envoy Count Nikolai Resanov as a follow-up to the earlier visit by Captain Laxman, who had returned Kodayu to Japan. Resanov came to Nagasaki to formally ask for the opening of trade relations between Japan and Russia, as had been suggested earlier by the Japanese authorities with whom Laxman had met. During Resanov's one-year stay in Nagasaki, the Russian made all kinds of trouble over ritual and etiquette, refusing to stand up when Japanese officials came to see him or to store his hand weapons as shogunal regulations required. Doeff was of some help to him, but as he had foreseen, the Russians were denied what they sought: the opening of trade with Japan. In G. H. von Langsdorff's *Journey around the World*, Captain Krusenstern describes his own and Resanov's frustrations, and here again we find Westerners agitated over a culturally attuned Dutchman—this time Doeff—who was bowing and scraping for the Japanese in the Japanese fashion.[69] Donald Keene, who apparently relishes this kind of condemnation for following local customs, quotes Krusenstern's litany in full: "How much it is regretted that an enlightened European nation, owing its political existence to a love of freedom, and which has acquired celebrity by great action, should so far debase itself from a desire of gains to attend with submission and devotion to the hateful commands of a set of slaves."[70]

In his own day, Doeff earned quite a reputation as the stubborn Dutch patriot who, with the connivance of the Japanese interpreters on Deshima, thrice withstood attempts by the English to make themselves master of the trade with Japan, and kept the Dutch flag flying on Deshima when elsewhere in the world it had been lowered. In October 1808, the British warship *Phaëton* paid a surprise visit to Nagasaki under the Dutch flag. Doeff succeeded in ushering her out of Nagasaki Bay before the local authorities discovered she was an English warship. In 1813 and 1814 he sabotaged two successive attempts by Thomas Stamford Raffles, lieutenant general of the British administration on

Celebration of two hundred years of friendship between Japan and the
Netherlands at Deshima, 1809. Artist: Kawahara Keiga. Collection of Nationaal
Scheepvaartmuseum, Amsterdam.

Java, to open up English trade with Japan. How all this happened is
told in detail in Doeff's *Recollections.*[71] Because of these risky exploits,
which he could carry out only with the aid of the local authorities
in Nagasaki, the "stubborn, lonesome exile on Deshima" was turned,
willy-nilly, into a nationalist icon. His heroic and romantic aura was
undoubtedly closely related to the turbulent and traumatic times in the
mother country.

The Netherlands were overrun by French troops in 1795 and subsequently turned into a client republic, the Batavian Republic. In 1806
the country was transformed into a kingdom, to provide Napoleon's el-
der brother, Louis Bonaparte, with a throne, and in 1810 it was incorporated into the French empire, until the French yoke was cast off in
November 1813 after Napoleon's defeat at the Battle of Leipzig. That
was not the end of the story, though, because in 1815 the survival of the
newly created kingdom of the Netherlands was challenged once more
at the Battle of Waterloo. Against this background of regime change,
the image of a lonely man living unperturbed on a far-away island,
hoisting and lowering the Dutch flag every day, must have been an
idyllic one indeed.

What concerns us here are other contributions that Doeff consciously made during his fifteen-year exile on Deshima. After he had thoroughly mastered the Japanese language, with the help of Japanese collaborators Doeff revised and rewrote the Dutch-Japanese dictionary, based on the original Dutch-French dictionary of François Halma. This great work, the *Doyaku-Haruma* (Halma Translated by Doeff), was used by all *rangakusha* until the 1850s, when the Dutch language gave way to English as the language for international studies. Fukuzawa Yukichi, who started his studies as a Dutch scholar, mentions how as a student he used to earn pocket money by copying the *Doyaku-Haruma* for wealthy patrons.

A lover of the Japanese language, Doeff also distinguished himself as an accomplished poet in the haiku genre. Well known is the short poem he devoted to a girl he watched cutting bean curd, on his way to the court in Edo:

> Inazuna no
> kaina wo karan
> kusamakura

> [Lend me your arms
> quick as lightning
> as pillows on my journey]

And if the following haiku, which he wrote while gazing over the wide expanse of Nagasaki Bay from the lookout post on top of his house, gives the impression he was a lazy fellow who spent his time dreamily waiting for ships that failed to show up, we now know that he actually kept himself busy teaching Dutch and French to the Japanese.

> Harukaze ya
> amakoma hashiru
> hokakebune

> [A spring breeze,
> to and fro they bustle
> the sailboats][72]

Hendrik Doeff's exile came to an end in 1817. He bade farewell to his female companion, Uryuno, and their nine-year-old son, Michitomi

Hendrik Doeff (1777–1835), in 1803. Artist: Kawahara Keiga. Collection of Kobe City Museum.

Yokichi, who were not allowed to leave with him, but he made sure of their financial well-being.[73] All his belongings, including an enormous collection of Japonalia, traveled with him to Batavia, and two years later he at long last left Java to sail home on the *De Ruyter,* one of the biggest ships of the fleet. Halfway across the Indian Ocean, in the neighborhood of the island of Diego Garcia, the ship sprang a leak and started sinking. The crew and passengers were rescued by an American brig, the *Pickering,* and Doeff had to watch helplessly as the *De Ruyter* went down with all his belongings. Thus his plan to commit himself upon his arrival in Holland to a study of Japan was dashed.

It would be another fifteen years before this modest man would decide to write his *Recollections of Japan*. Although he had read the denunciations of Dutch behavior by Krusenstern and the bitter reproaches by Lady Raffles in *The Life and Public Service of Sir Thomas Stamford Raffles*, it was not until 1830 that he was moved to action.[74] In that year, Philipp Franz von Siebold returned to the Netherlands with an enormous collection of Japanese artifacts and entered the service of the king to embark on his great project, *Nippon*—an enterprise that would remain uncompleted after twenty years of work. Von Siebold and the storehouse master of Deshima, J. F. van Overmeer Fischer, who also sold his collection of artifacts to the king, announced with some fanfare that they had composed a Dutch-Japanese dictionary. As soon as Doeff heard about this, he protested vehemently, because he knew that they had probably used the copy that he had left behind on Deshima. This prompted him to write his *Recollections*, as a way to set straight all the slights he had suffered over the years.[75]

Epilogue

In this volume and in my original Reischauer Lectures, my purpose was to explore, by using three port cities as heuristic tools, how European traders' expansion into the maritime sphere of East and Southeast Asia was concomitant with the spread of private traders from south China, who swarmed out all over the China Seas, and also what impact the great global political and industrial revolutions of the 1780s and 1790s had on the China Seas region. I have called Batavia, Canton, and Nagasaki "visible cities" not only because they are represented visually in maps and drawings of the time more than any other cities in Asia, but also because they laid bare the regional impact of global developments. But were these three cities simply variations on the same theme, like the "invisible cities" in Marco Polo's tales to the Great Khan in Italo Calvino's novel?

Each of these old-world emporiums represented a deliberate effort by the political economy it served to gain a firm grip on international trade; witness the continuous development of checks and balances designed to manage the shifts in maritime traffic over the years. Batavia, designed as a rendezvous to serve the seaborne empire of the VOC in Monsoon Asia, had a complicated corpus of tariffs and regulations and met its self-inflicted demise when trade on the periphery of that empire turned in other directions (although it was, at least temporarily, bailed out by the arrival of the Americans). In Nagasaki, the *bakufu* almost stifled overseas trade as it held on to Japan's autarkic policies, but the door was left ajar for the purpose of gathering information about the outside world. There, too, the American traders arrived like a gallant knight on a white horse.

Only in Canton did the sky seem the limit in terms of trade, even though the character of the Western presence in the region was changing. While company monopolies were giving way to the private enterprise of country traders and the newly arrived Americans, the Canton system itself—in which the Hong merchants operated by proxy for the imperial administration to contain the Western traders (another complicated system of checks and balances)—remained basically intact. This system eased negotiations in the marketplace but not the imbalance of trade, and certainly not the political issues that were at stake. It must have been clear to all participants, as the situation along the China Coast quickly deteriorated, that the opium-for-tea trade would not last forever, but short-term profits overshadowed any kind of reasoning among those involved in the extremely lucrative business. The Bostonians told themselves it remained, indeed, "a fair, honorable, and legitimate trade."

There can be no doubt that the effects of global change were wrenching for the trade of the South China Sea. The seascape that had been for so long an inner sea, self-contained in terms of trade, became increasingly connected to the rapidly expanding global economy. Although all European participants in the Far Eastern trade, with the exception of the British, had to withdraw from the market during the 1790s owing to the war with the French, they were quickly replaced by Americans. Even while Europe was at war, global trade continued to expand.

It briefly looked as though the Europeans' loss was the Americans' gain. Dutch consul Pieter van Berckel's fear that the Americans would start sending large numbers of ships to the Orient was confirmed, and his prediction that they might turn into rivals in trade was fulfilled. But ironically the American traders were a blessing in disguise. When Dutch ships could no longer reach Batavia, Canton, and Nagasaki as a result of the Napoleonic Wars, in rode the Yankees on their white-sailed vessels to bail out the Dutch trading settlements in Asia that were stuck with large quantities of goods they could not ship out. Then the Americans had to withdraw when Thomas Jefferson imposed his infamous Embargo Act in 1807. The British made several vain attempts to take advantage of this situation—and even threatened to occupy Macao—until the Chinese forced them to withdraw.

One wonders how the United States' scramble for the Asian trade would have developed without Jefferson's American version of Napoleon's Continental System. It is simply impossible to render any kind of judgment in terms of winners and losers in the year 1807–08. History does not even show a "draw" that year among the parties involved—it was basically a time-out. One thing is crystal clear, however: the old regime among Western traders in Asia had come to an end.

Lately it has been fashionable among students of Southeast Asian history—and I would like to stress the history of *mainland* Southeast Asia—to argue that the period between 1750 and 1780 represented a kind of crisis out of which a new and modern order was born. Anthony Reid and Victor Lieberman even speak of "the last stand of Asian autonomy."[76] I am not so sure we can say the same of the situation in the maritime sphere, where everything was in flux and very much out of control.[77] It is true that the governments of China and Japan made a stand for tradition, but neither formulated a coherent response to the challenges of modernity.

It is certainly difficult to discern any new order in Southeast Asian waters, where interlopers, country traders, pirates, and smugglers threw into question all prior power relations without really replacing them. It is probably safe to say that we cannot speak of the birth of a new era in maritime trade until a new type of port city emerged on the rim of the South China Sea that would serve the particular needs and demands of the Chinese trading network in the area. Thomas Stamford Raffles's brilliant decision to articulate the changing global trade with the expanding overseas Chinese economy by establishing a new kind of emporium, the *free port* of Singapore, was the first step in that new direction. And when from 1842 Hong Kong, Shanghai, Yokohama, Kobe, and all the other treaty ports followed, a new situation in international trade indeed emerged. Canton and Nagasaki, the exclusive emporiums of old, were no longer controlled by the central governments of China and Japan. How that came about is a completely different and complex story, and for those who really want to know, I have only one recommendation: read John King Fairbank![78]

Notes
Bibliography
Index

Notes

1. Three Windows of Opportunity

1. *Ideal Commonwealths: Comprising, More's Utopia, Bacon's New Atlantis, Campanella's City of the Sun, and Harriton's Oceana*, P. F. Collier and Son; New York: The Colonial Press, 1914. Sir Thomas More, *Utopia*, 2nd ed., trans. Robert Adams, New York: W. W. Norton, 1992. See also *http://oregonstate.edu/instruct/phl302/texts/more/utopia-contents.html*.

2. Italo Calvino, *Invisible Cities*, trans. William Weaver, New York: Harcourt Brace Jovanovich, 1974.

3. Among the sources I cite here just a few titles. For Canton see: Paul Van Dyke, *The Canton Trade: Life and Enterprise on the China Coast 1700–1845*, Hong Kong: Hongkong University Press, 2005; Louis Dermigny, *La Chine et l'occident: Le commerce à Canton au 18e siècle, 1719–1833*, Paris: SEVPEN, 1964, 3 vols. For Batavia see: Leonard Blussé, *Strange Company: Chinese Settlers, Mestizo Women, and the Dutch in VOC Batavia*, Dordrecht, Holland: Foris Publications, 1986; F. de Haan, *Oud Batavia*, Bandung, Indonesia: A. C. Nix, 1935, 2 vols.; H. E. Niemeijer, *Batavia: Een koloniale samenleving in de zeventiende eeuw*, Amsterdam: Balans Publishers, 2005. For Nagasaki see: Nagasaki City Government (ed.), *Nagasaki shishi*, Nagasaki: Nagasaki Shiyakusho, 1923–1935, 8 vols.; Yamawaki Teijirō, *Nagasaki no Oranda shōkan: Sekai no naka no sakoku Nihon*, Tokyo: Chūō Kōronsha, 1980; Yamawaki Teijirō, *Nagasaki no Tōjin bōeki*, Tokyo: Yoshikawa Kōbunkan, 1964.

4. Edwin O. Reischauer and John King Fairbank, *East Asia: The Great Tradition*, Boston: Houghton Mifflin, 1960; John King Fairbank, Edwin O. Reischauer, and Albert M. Craig, *East Asia: The Modern Transformation*, Boston: Houghton Mifflin, 1965.

5. John King Fairbank, *Trade and Diplomacy on the China Coast: The Opening of the Treaty Ports 1842–1854*. Stanford, CA: Stanford University Press, 1969; Edwin

Reischauer, *Ennin's Travels in T'ang China*, New York: Ronald Press Company, 1955.

6. On March 20, 1602, the States-General of the Dutch Republic granted the United East India Company, or Verenigde Oost-Indische Compagnie (VOC), a charter for the trade monopoly in the East Indies. The Company was dissolved in 1798 when all its assets and liabilities were taken over by the Batavian Republic.

7. Most of the *dagregisters*, or diaries, of Batavia in the seventeenth century have appeared in print. Over the past thirty years the Historiographical Institute of Tokyo University has been publishing the transcriptions of the original Dutch versions and their Japanese translation in a slow but meticulous manner; see Historiographical Institute (ed.), *Oranda Shokancho Nikki: Diaries Kept by the Heads of the Dutch Factory in Japan, 1633–1647* [Original Dutch Texts], vols. 1–10 (1974–2003); Japanese translation, vols. 1–10 (1976–2004). The so-called marginalia versions have been published in English, covering all diaries of the eighteenth century. Paul van der Velde and Rudolf Bachofner (eds.), *The Deshima Diaries Marginalia 1700–1740*, Tokyo: Japan-Netherlands Institute, 1992; Leonard Blussé et al. (eds.), *The Deshima Diaries Marginalia 1740–1800*, Tokyo: Japan-Netherlands Institute, 2004. At present the marginalia of the diaries of the seventeenth century are being translated and annotated in English. Cynthia Viallé and Leonard Blussé, *The Deshima Dagregisters 1640–1660*, Intercontinenta Series No. 23 and 25, Leiden: IGEER, 2001, 2005, 2 vols. Recently the English translation of the extant eighteenth-century diaries of the Dutch factory in Guangzhou (Canton) has been initiated by the Cultural Institute of Macao.

8. It is of course impossible to include or refer to all these data here. I can only hope that this volume will raise the interest of those historians of Monsoon Asia who have never made use of the VOC archive or its source publications. For the inventory of the VOC archives preserved in the National Archive at The Hague, see: M. A. P. Meilink-Roelofsz, R. Raben, and H. Spijkerman (eds.), *De archieven van de Verenigde Oostindische Compagnie/The Archives of the Dutch East India Company (1602–1795), History and Manual*, The Hague: Sdu Uitgeverij Koninginnegracht, 1992.

9. Philip A. Kuhn, *Origins of the Modern Chinese State*, Stanford, CA: Stanford University Press, 2002.

10. "No criteria exist to set the port city apart from the city in general or from a port as such, or a coastal town or village. Physically functioning as a port, a place where trade goods or passengers were exchanged between land and sea . . . port cities might often have the distinct character of a maritime community and serve as agents of social, cultural, and economic interchange." Peter G. Reeves, *Ports and Port Cities as Places of Social Interaction in the Indian Ocean Region: A Preliminary Historical Bibliography*, Perth: Centre for South and Southeast Asian Studies, University of Western Australia, 1981.

11. Fernand Braudel, *Civilization and Capitalism, 15th–18th century*, 1st U.S. ed., New York: Harper & Row, 1982–1984, 3 vols.

12. Frank Broeze (ed.), *Brides of the Sea: Port Cities of Asia from the 16th–20th Centuries*, Honolulu: University of Hawaii Press, 1989. Frank Broeze (ed.), in association with the Asian Studies Association of Australia, *Gateways of Asia: Port Cities of Asia in the 13th–20th centuries*, New York: Kegan Paul International, 1997.

13. Rekishigaku Kenkyukai, *Minatomachi no sekkaishi* [Port Cities in World History], Tokyo: Aoki Shoten Publishing, 2005, 3 vols.

14. K. N. Chaudhuri, *The Trading World of Asia and the English East India Company, 1660–1760*, Cambridge: Cambridge University Press, 1978.

15. Angela Schottenhammer (ed.), *Trade and Transfer across the East Asian "Mediterranean,"* Wiesbaden: Harrassowitz, 2005.

16. John King Fairbank (ed.), *The Chinese World Order: Traditional China's Foreign Relations*, Cambridge, MA: Harvard University Press, 1968. J. E. Wills, "Qing Relations with Annam and Siam, 1680–1810," paper prepared for presentation at the 18th IAHA Conference, Taipei, December 2004.

17. Hans Bielenstein, *Diplomacy and Trade in the Chinese World, 589–1276*, Leiden: Brill, 2005, pp. 4, 5, 675.

18. See, for instance, Alain Peyrefitte's remarks on this issue in his introduction to this Chinese correspondence. Alain Peyrefitte and Pierre Henri Durand, *Un choc de cultures, la vision des Chinois,* Paris: Fayard 1991, p. lxxii.

19. Jane Kate Leonard, *Wei Yuan and China's Rediscovery of the Maritime World*, Cambridge, MA: Harvard University Press, 1984.

20. Liu Xicheng in his preface to Wang Daihai's *Haidao yizhi*, translated by W. H. Medhurst as *Chinaman Abroad; Desultory Account of the Malayan Archipelago*, Shanghai, 1849, p. viii.

21. Tian Rukang, "Shiqi shiji zhi shijiu shiji zhongye Zhongguo fanchuan zai Dongnan Yazhou hangyun he shangye shangdi diwei" [The Position of Chinese Shipping in the Maritime Trade of Southeast Asia from the Seventeenth until the Nineteenth Century], *Lishi Yanjiu* VIII (1956), pp. 1–21, and XII (1957), pp. 1–12, both published in Tian Rukang, *Zhongguo fan chuan mao yi he dui wai guanxi shi lun ji* [A Collection of Historical Essays on the Trade of Chinese Sailing Ships and Foreign Relations], Hangzhou: Zhejiang renmin chuban she, 1987. See also T'ien Ju-k'ang, "The Chinese Junk Trade: Merchants, Entrepreneurs, and Coolies, 1600–1850," in Klaus Friedland (ed.), *Maritime Aspects of Migration*, Cologne: Böhlau, 1987, pp. 381–389.

22. Several studies on specific aspects of the early modern Chinese maritime trading network have appeared recently. Chen Xiyu has described the shipping enterprise, in *Zhongguo fanchuan yu haiwai maoyi* [Chinese Sailing Ships and Overseas Trade], Xiamen: n.p., 1991. A very detailed account of the organization of early Dongxi-yang shipping is provided in Lin Renchuan, *Fujian dui haiwai maoyi yu haiguanshi* [The History of Fujian's Overseas Trade and the Customs], Xiamen: Lujiang chubanshe, 1991. Post-1680 trade in Amoy (Xiamen) is described in Ng Chin-Keong, *Trade and Society: The Amoy Network on the China Coast, 1683–1735*, Singapore: Singapore University Press, 1983. For the Siamese trade with China, see Jennifer W. Cushman, *Fields from the Sea: Chinese Junk Trade with Siam during the Late Eighteenth and Early Nineteenth Centuries*, Ithaca: Cornell University Press, 1975. The history of the junk trade to Batavia is described in Blussé, *Strange Company*, pp. 97–155. The Fujianese network is described in James Chin Kong, "Merchants and Other Sojourners: The Hokkien Overseas, 1570–1760," PhD diss., University of Hong Kong, 1998, and Liao Dage, *Fujian haiwai jiaotongshi* [A General History of the Maritime Trade of Fujian], Fuzhou: Fujian renmin chubanshe, 2002.

23. See, for instance, Sarasin Viraphol, *Tribute and Profit: Sino-Siamese Trade, 1652–1853*, Cambridge, MA: Harvard University Press, 1977, and Hamashita Takeshi, *Kindai chūgoku no kokusaiteki keiki: Chōkō bōeki shisutemu to kindai Ajia* [Early Modern China's International Turning Points: The Tribute Trade System and Early Modern Asia], Tokyo: Tokyo Daigaku Shuppankai, 1990.

24. Kuwabara Jitsuzo, "On P'u Shou-keng," *Memoirs of the Research Department of the Toyo Bunko* 2 (1928), pp. 1–79; vol. 7 (1935), pp. 1–104; Billy K. L. So, *Prosperity, Region, and Institutions in Maritime China: The South Fukien Pattern, 946–1368*, Cambridge, MA: Harvard University Press, 2000.

25. Bodo Wiethoff, *Die chinesische Seeverbotspolitik und der private Überseehandel von 1368 bis 1567*, Hamburg: Gesellschaft für Natur- und Völkerkunde Ostasiens, 1963.

26. Chang Pin-tsun, "Maritime Trade and Local Economy in Late Ming Fukien," in E. B. Vermeer (ed.), *Development and Decline of Fukien Province in the 17th and 18th Centuries*, Leiden: Brill, 1990, p. 66.

27. Chang, Pin-tsun, "Chinese Maritime Trade: The Case of Sixteenth-Century Fu-chien," PhD diss., Princeton University, 1983.

28. The Dongxi-yang maritime route system was extensively described in 1617 by the Fujianese literatus Zhang Xie (1574–1640), in all its aspects: succinct descriptions of the ports along the way, with their specific products; the navigational route itself; the organization of the crews on board; the tax system; and related literary essays. Zhang Xie, *Dong xi yang kao* [A Treatise on the Eastern and Western Oceans], Beijing: Zhonghua shuju, 1981.

29. Femme S. Gaastra, *The Dutch East India Company: Expansion and Decline*, Zutphen: De Walburg Pers, 2003.

30. For a survey of the history of Dutch-Japanese relations, see Leonard Blussé, Willem Remmelink, and Ivo Smits (eds.), *Bridging the Divide: 400 Years, the Netherlands-Japan*, Hilversum: Teleac/NOT and Hotei Publishing, 2000.

31. F. Valentijn, *Oud en Nieuw Oost-Indiën* [Old and New East Indies], Dordrecht: J. van Braam, 1724–1726, vol. 5b, p. 165.

32. Leonard Blussé, "Divesting a Myth: Seventeenth-Century Dutch-Portuguese Rivalry in the Far East," in Anthony Disney and Emily Booth (eds.), *Vasco da Gama and the Linking of Europe and Asia*, New Delhi: Oxford University Press, 2000, pp. 387–402.

33. Historiographical Institute, *Oranda Shôkancho Nikki: Diaries Kept by the Heads of the Dutch Factory in Japan*, Original Text Selection 1, vol. 4, 26 July 1639, pp. 60–61.

34. Leonard Blussé, "Amongst Feigned Friends and Declared Enemies," in Solvi Sogner (ed.), *Making Sense of Global History*, Oslo: Universitetsforlaget, 2002, p. 163.

35. Gentlemen Seventeen to J. P. Coen, 14 April 1622, quoted in Niels Steensgaard, "The Dutch East India Company as an Institutional Innovation," in Maurice Aymar (ed.), *Dutch Capitalism and World Capitalism*, Cambridge: Cambridge University Press, 1977, p. 255.

36. Manuscript H45, KITLV (Royal Institute for Anthropology) Library, Leiden, *Patriase missive*, 19 September 1633.

37. Gang Zhao, "Reshaping the Asian Trade Network: The Construction and Execution of the 1684 Chinese Open Trade Policies," PhD diss., John Hopkins University, 2006.

38. John E. Wills, *Pepper, Guns, and Parleys: The Dutch East India Company and China, 1662–1681*, Cambridge, MA: Harvard University Press, 1974.

39. For a case study of Dutch administrative control of the junk trade at Batavia, see "The VOC and the Junk Trade to Batavia: A Problem in Administrative Control," in Blussé, *Strange Company*. About the particular restrictions mentioned here, see p. 127.

2. Managing Trade across Cultures

1. The source for the epigraph is Italo Calvino, *Invisible Cities*, trans. William Weaver, New York: Harcourt Brace Jovanovich, 1974, "Trading Cities," p. 51.

2. Leonard Blussé, "Brief Encounter at Macao," special issue: essays dedicated to Charles Boxer, *Modern Asian Studies* 22, no. 3 (1988): 647–663.

3. Kenneth McPherson, "Port Cities as Nodal Points of Change: The Indian Ocean, 1890s–1920s," in *Modernity and Culture: From the Mediterranean to the Indian Ocean*, Leila Tarazi Fawaz and C. A. Bayly (eds.), New York: Columbia University Press, 2002, pp. 75–76.

4. Bhawan Ruangsilp, *Dutch East India Company Merchants at the Court of Ayutthaya: Dutch Perceptions of the Thai Kingdom, c. 1604–1765*, TANAP Monographs on the History of Asian-European Interaction 8, Leiden: Brill, 2007.

5. Leonard Blussé, "Amongst Feigned Friends and Declared Enemies," in Solvi Sogner (ed.), *Making Sense of Global History*, Oslo: Universitetsforlaget, 2002, pp. 154–168.

6. Niels Steensgaard, "The Dutch East India Company as an Institutional Innovation," in Maurice Aymar (ed.), *Dutch Capitalism and World Capitalism*, New York: Cambridge University Press, 1977, p. 255. Also in Pieter Emmer and Femme Gaastra (eds.), *The Organization of Inter-oceanic Trade in European Expansion, 1450–1800*, London: Variorum 1996, p. 153.

7. Blair B. Kling and M. N. Pearson (eds.), *The Age of Partnership: Europeans in Asia before Dominion*, Honolulu: University of Hawaii Press, 1979.

8. Leonard Blussé, "No Boats to China: The Dutch East India Company and the Changing Pattern of the China Sea Trade, 1635–1690," *Modern Asian Studies* 30, no. 1 (1996): 51–76.

9. Hendrik E. Niemeijer, *Batavia: Een koloniale samenleving in de zeventiende eeuw*, Amsterdam: Balans, 2005.

10. Remco Raben, "Round about Batavia: Ethnicity and Authority in the Ommelanden, 1650–1800," in K. Grijns and Peter J. M. Nas (eds.), *Jakarta-Batavia: Socio-cultural Essays*, Leiden: KITLV Press, 2000, pp. 93–113.

11. H. Kroeskamp, "De Chinezen te Batavia (1700) als exempel voor de Christenen van West Europa," *Indonesië* 6, no. 4 (1953): 346–371.

12. Leonard Blussé, "Queen among Kings: Diplomatic Ritual at Batavia," in Grijns and Nas (eds.), *Jakarta-Batavia*, pp. 25–42.

13. Leonard Blussé, "The Vicissitudes of Maritime Trade: Letters from the Ocean Merchant, Li Kunhe, to the Dutch Authorities in Batavia (1803–09)," in Anthony Reid (ed.), *Sojourners and Settlers: Histories of Southeast Asia and the Chinese*, St. Leonards, Australia: Allen and Unwin, 1996.

14. Leonard Blussé, *Strange Company: Chinese Settlers, Mestizo Women, and the Dutch in VOC Batavia*, Dordrecht: Foris Publications, 1986, pp. 73–96.

15. Leonard Blussé and Chen Menghong (eds.), *The Archives of the Kong Koan of Batavia*, Leiden: Brill, 2003.

16. The tael was part of the Chinese weight system and denoted in currency about forty grams of silver.

17. Fu Lo-shu, *A Documentary Chronicle of Sino-Western Relations*, Tucson: University of Arizona Press, 1966, p. 174.

18. "The Story of an Ecological Disaster: The Dutch East India Company and Batavia (1619–1799)," in Blussé, *Strange Company*, pp. 15–34.

19. P. H. van der Brug, *Malaria en malaise: De VOC in Batavia in de achttiende eeuw,* Amsterdam: De Bataafsche Leeuw, 1994.

20. Isaac Titsingh, *The Private Correspondence of Isaac Titsingh,* ed. Frank Lequin, Amsterdam: J. C. Gieben, 1990, vol. 1, p. 245.

21. For an all-encompassing account of the town's earlier history, see Geoffrey C. Gunn, *Nagasaki in the Asian Bullion Trade Networks,* Tonan Ajiakenkyu sōsho [Southeast Asian Research Series] no. 32, Nagasaki: Nagasaki daigaku keizaibu Tonan-ajia kenkyujo, 1999.

22. Ibid., p. 62.

23. One particular *opperhoofd* carefully noted down where and with whom he slept during his court journey to Edo. See Letter by H. C. Romberg to I. Titsingh in Titsingh, *Private Correspondence of Isaac Titsingh,* vol. 2, pp. 698–699; also pp. 702, 704, 707, and elsewhere.

24. Engelbert Kaempfer, *The Furthest Goal: Engelbert Kaempfer's Encounter with Tokugawa Japan,* ed. Beatrice M. Bodart-Bailey and Derek Massarella, Folkestone, Kent: Japan Library, 1995; L. Blussé et al. (eds.), *The Deshima Diaries Marginalia 1740–1800,* Tokyo: Japan-Netherlands Institute 2004, passim.

25. Cees Camfferman and Terence E. Cooke, "The Profits of the Dutch East India Company's Japan Trade," *Abacus* 40, no. 1 (2004): 49–75.

26. Ryuto Shimada, *The Intra-Asian Trade in Japanese Copper by the Dutch East India Company during the Eighteenth Century,* TANAP Monographs on the History of Asian-European Interaction 4, Leiden: Brill, 2006, pp. 39–44.

27. Iwao Seiichi et al. (eds.), *Oranda fūsetsugaki shūsei* [A Compilation of the Dutch News Reports], Tokyo: Yoshikawa Kōbunkan, 1977–1979, 2 vols. Matsukata Fuyuko, "1660-nendai fūsetsugaki no kakuritsu katei" [The Formalization Process of Fusetsugaki in the 1660s], in Fujita Satoru (ed.), *17-seiki no Nihon to Higashi Ajia* [Seventeenth-Century Japan and the West], Tokyo: Yamakawa Shuppensha, 2000. Matsukata Fuyuko, *Oranda Fusetsugaki to Kinsei Nihon* [The Dutch World News and Early Modern Japan], Tokyo: Tokyo University Press, 2007.

28. Marius B. Jansen, "Rangaku and Westernization," *Modern Asian Studies* 18, no. 4 (1984): 542.

29. Shizuki, also called Nakano Ryuho (1760–1806), was a former interpreter on Deshima. He studied Willem Sewel's *Nederduytse Spraakkonst,* a Dutch grammar of 1708 (republished many times) and wrote *Oranda Shihinko* [A Study of Dutch Parts of Speech].

30. Engelbert Kaempfer, "An Enquiry, whether it be conducive for the good of the Japanese Empire, to keep it shut up, as it is now, and not to suffer its inhabitants to have any Commerce with foreign nations, either at home or abroad," in E. Kaempfer, *The History of Japan,* repr., Richmond, Surrey: Curzon Press, 1993, vol. 3, p. 330.

31. Hosea Ballou Morse, *The Chronicles of the East India Company Trading to China 1635–1834,* Cambridge, MA, 1926. Earl Hampton Pritchard, *The Crucial Years of Early Anglo-Chinese Relations, 1750–1800,* Research Studies of the State College of Washington, vol. 4, nos. 3–4, Washington: Pullman, 1937. Paul A. Van Dyke, *The Canton Trade: Life and Enterprise on the China Coast 1700–1845,* Hong Kong: Hongkong University Press, 2005.

32. Erik Gobel, "The Danish Asiatic Company's Voyages to China 1732–1833," *Scandinavian Economic History Review* 27, no. 1 (1979): 11. Foster Rhea Dulles, *The Old China Trade,* New York: AMS Press 1930, p. 12.

33. Van Dyke, *The Canton Trade*, p. 12.

34. Jacques M. Downs, *The Golden Ghetto: The American Commercial Community at Canton and the Shaping of American China Policy, 1784–1844*, Bethlehem, PA: Lehigh University Press, 1997, p. 392, n. 175: "We rowed through streets at least 1–1½ miles; on each side was the boat population of Canton and through the center were passing to & fro boats 20 times more numerous & with less confusion than the omnibuses & carriages in Broadway opposite the Astor House."

35. William Hickey, *Memoirs of William Hickey*, ed. Peter Quennell, London: Routledge and Kegan Paul, 1975, p. 136.

36. Carter Goodrich (comp.), *The Government and the Economy, 1783–1861*, Indianapolis: Bobbs-Merrill 1967, pp. 337–339, 348. With thanks to Frederic Grant, who pointed this out to me.

37. Dulles, *The Old China Trade*, p. 20.

38. Ibid., p. 21.

39. Henry Hobhouse, *Seeds of Change: Six Plants That Transformed Mankind*, London: Papermac, 1999, p. 115.

40. Van Dyke, *The Canton Trade*, pp. 146–147.

41. Robert L. Irick, *Ch'ing Policy toward the Coolie Trade 1847–1878*, Taipei: CMC Publishing, 1982. p. 13.

42. Tian Rukang, *Zhongguo fan chuan mao yi he dui wai guanxi shi lun ji* [A Collection of Historical Essays on the Trade of Chinese Sailing Ships and Foreign Relations], Hangzhou: Zhejiang renmin chuban she, 1987, p. 16.

43. Blussé, *Strange Company*, p. 134–135.

44. Carl Trocki, "Chinese Pioneering in Eighteenth-Century Southeast Asia," in Anthony Reid (ed.), *The Last Stand of Asian Autonomies*, New York: Macmillan, 1997, p. 87.

45. National Archives, The Hague, VOC 172, 28 November 1752. Liu Yong, *The Dutch East India Company's Tea Trade with China, 1757–1781*, TANAP Monographs on the History of Asian-European Interaction 6, Leiden: Brill, 2007, pp. 17–41.

46. See J. de Hullu, "De instelling van de commissie voor den handel der Oost-Indische Compagnie op China in 1756," *Bijdragen tot de Taal-, Land-, en Volkenkunde van Nederlandsch-Indië*, KITLV, (1923): 529–533, and Liu, *The Dutch East India Company's Tea Trade with China*, p. 23.

47. James Francis Warren, *The Global Economy and the Sulu Zone: Connections, Commodities, and Culture*, Quezon City, Philippines: New Day Publishers, 2000. James Francis Warren, *Iranun and Balaningi Globalization, Maritime Raiding and the Birth of Ethnicity*, Singapore: Singapore University Press, 2002.

48. "Voorschriften op de vaart en handel der Chinese jonken," in J. A. van der Chijs, *Nederlandsch-Indisch Plakaatboek 1602–1811*, Batavia: Landsdrukkerij, 1885–1900, vol. 10, p. 227, 9 April 1778.

49. Ibid., vol. 11, p. 618, "Adres Isaac Titsingh van 24 september 1793."

50. Dulles, *The Old China Trade*, p. 11.

51. Downs, *The Golden Ghetto*. Jonathan Goldstein, *Philadelphia and the China Trade 1682–1846: Commercial, Cultural and Attitudinal Effects*, University Park: Pennsylvania State University Press, 1978. Kenneth Scott Latourette, *The History of Early Relations between the United States and China, 1784–1844*, New Haven: Yale University Press, 1917.

52. Fu, *A Documentary Chronicle of Sino-Western Relations*, p. 303.

53. It is good to know that there is a scholar who is doing precisely this. See James Fichter, "American East Indies, 1773–1815," PhD diss., Harvard University, 2006.

54. William Bentley, *The Diary of William Bentley, D.D., Pastor of the East Church, Salem, Massachusetts, 1784–December 1819*, Salem, MA: Essex Institute, 1905; repr., Gloucester, MA: Peter Smith, 1962, 4 vols.

55. Benjamin Franklin: In Search of a Better World, December 2005–April 2006, National Constitution Center, Philadelphia.

56. Amasa Delano, *Delano's Voyages of Commerce and Discovery: Amasa Delano in China, the Pacific Islands, Australia, and South America, 1789–1807*, Stockbridge, MA: Berkshire House Publishers, 1994. (Original title: *A Narrative of Voyages and Travels in the Northern and Southern Hemispheres.*)

57. Jeffrey A. Frankel, "The 1807–1809 Embargo against Great Britain," *Journal of Economic History* 42, no. 2 (June 1982): 291–308.

58. J. de Hullu, "On the Rise of the Indies Trade of the United States of America as Competitor of the East India Company in the Period 1786–1790," in M. A. P. Meilink-Roelofsz (ed.), *Dutch Authors on Asian History*, Dordrecht: KITLV, 1988, p. 144.

59. There is no room here to discuss this important subject, but the sudden rise of piracy in the coastal waters of Guangdong Province has been studied in detail by Dian Murray, *Pirates of the South China Coast, 1790–1810*, Stanford: Stanford University Press 1987, and Robert J. Antony, *Like Froth Floating on the Sea: The World of Pirates and Seafarers in Late Imperial South China*, Berkeley, CA: Institute of East Asian Studies, 2003. Curiously, neither has looked at the role that opium smuggling may have played in the emergence of this wave of piracy.

60. Nicholas B. Dirks, *The Scandal of Empire: India and the Creation of Imperial Britain*, Cambridge, MA: Belknap Press of Harvard University Press, 2006.

61. About the recalcitrant behavior of one particular British country trader, John McClary, see Liu, *The Dutch East India Company's Tea Trade with China*, pp. 111–117.

3. Bridging the Divide

1. E. H. P. Baudet, *Paradise on Earth: Some Thoughts on European Images of Non-European Man*, Westport, CT: Greenwood Press, 1976.

2. Peter Heath, "War and Peace in the Works of Erasmus: A Medieval Perspective," in Andrew Ayton and J. L. Price (eds.), *The Medieval Military Revolution: State, Society and Military Change in Medieval and Early Modern Europe*, London: I. B. Taurus Publishers, p. 121.

3. Frederik van Heek, *Chineesche Immigranten in Nederland*, Amsterdam: J. Emmering, 1936.

4. The vicissitudes of these bands have been well described by Dian H. Murray, *Pirates of the South China Coast, 1790–1810*, Stanford: Stanford University Press, 1987; Robert Antony, *Like Froth Floating on the Sea: The World of Pirates and Seafarers in Late Imperial South China*, Berkeley, CA: Institute of East Asian Studies, 2003; and James Francis Warren, *Iranun and Balanigni: Globalization, Maritime Raiding and the Birth of Ethnicity*, Kent Ridge, Singapore: Singapore University Press, 2002.

5. Leonard Blussé, *Bitter Bonds: A Colonial Divorce Drama of the Seventeenth Century*, Princeton, NJ: Markus Wiener Publishers, 2002.

6. William Hickey, *Memoirs of William Hickey*, ed. Peter Quennell, London: Routledge and Keegan Paul, 1975, p. 123.

7. M. A. P. Meilink-Roelofsz, "Ulrich Gualtherus Hemmingson, V.O.C. dienaar en verbindingsschakel tussen China en Nederland," *Nederlands Kunsthistorisch Jaarboek* 31 (1980): 469.

8. Frits Vos, "Forgotten Foibles: Love and the Dutch on Deshima," in *Asien, Tradition und Fortschritt; Festschrift für Horst Hammitzsch*, Wiesbaden: O. Harrassowitz, 1971, p. 622.

9. Yung Lun yuen, *History of the Pirates Who Infested the China Sea from 1807 to 1810*, translated from the Chinese original with notes and illustrations by Charles Fried, London: Neumann, 1831.

10. *Gongan bu, Bacheng huaren Gongguan Dangan* [Minutes of the Board Meetings of the Chinese Council of Batavia], Xiamen: Xiamen University Press, 2002, vol. 1, p. 1.

11. Laura Hostetler, *Qing Colonial Enterprise: Ethnography and Cartography in Early Modern China*, Chicago: University of Chicago Press, 2001, p. 5.

12. Ong-Dae-Hae [Wang Dahai], *The Chinaman Abroad: or a Desultory Account of the Malayan Archipelago, Particularly of Java*, trans. W. H. Medhurst, Shanghai, 1848, pp. 5–6.

13. Ibid., p. 6.

14. Ibid., pp. 6–7. See also Claudine Salmon, "Wang Dahai et sa vision des 'contrées insulaires,'" *Etudes Chinoises* 8, no. 1–2 (1994).

15. Luo Fangbo, "Rhapsody on My Travels to Gold Mountain," excerpted from Yuan Bingling, *Chinese Democracies, a Study of the Kongsis of West Borneo (1776–1884)*, CNWS Publications 79, Leiden: Research School CNWS, Leiden University, 2000, pp. 302–303.

16. Wilt Idema, "Vreemde bedden en een grabbelton," *Armada* 19 (2000): 28, 29.

17. Donald Keene, *The Japanese Discovery of Europe, 1720–1830*, rev. ed., Stanford: Stanford University Press, 1969, p. 23.

18. Martha Chaiklin, *Cultural Commerce and Dutch Commercial Culture: The Influence of European Material Culture on Japan, 1700–1850*, Studies in Overseas History 5, Leiden: CNWS Press, 2003; Timon Screech, *The Lens within the Heart: The Western Scientific Gaze and Popular Imagery in Later Edo Japan*, Honolulu: University of Hawaii Press, 2002; Calvin L. French, *Shiba Kōkan: Pioneer of Western Art and Sciences in Japan*, New York, 1966.

19. Keene, *Japanese Discovery*, p. 6.

20. Grant Kohn Goodman, *Japan and the Dutch, 1600–1853*, Richmond, Surrey: Curzon Press, 2000, p. 85.

21. Klaus Müller, "Shiba Kokan und sein Seiyo-gadan als Beispiel für die Entstehung kunstfremder Einflüsse in der westlichen Malerei der Edo-Zeit," in Lydia Brüll and Ulrich Kemper (eds.), *Asien, Tradition und Fortschritt: Festschrift für Horst Hammitzsch zu seinem 60. Geburtstag*, Wiesbaden: O. Harrassowitz, 1971, pp. 416–431.

22. Shiba Kōkan, *Edo, Nagasaki e kikō: Saiyū ryotan*, Tokyo: Kokusho Kankōkai, 1992; Shiba Kōkan, *Kōkan saiyū nikki*, ed. Haga Tōru and Ōta Rieko, Tokyo: Heibonsha, 1986.

23. She is actually the same lady whose seventeen-year tug-of-war with her Dutch second husband, Joan Bitter, in Batavia has been described in *Bitter Bonds*; see n. 5.

24. Donald Keene, *Travelers of a Hundred Ages*, New York: H. Holt and Co., 1989, p. 364.

25. Keene, *Japanese Discovery*, pp. 9, 12.

26. Frank Lequin, *Isaac Titsingh (1745–1812), een passie voor Japan: Leven en werk van de grondlegger van de Europese Japanologie*, Alphen aan den Rijn: Canaletto/Repro-Holland, 2002. Timon Screech, *Secret Memoirs of the Shoguns: Isaac Titsingh and Japan, 1779–1822*. New York: Routledge, 2006.

27. Edward Roberts Barnsley, *The First VBH: A biography about the remarkable life of an eighteenth-century Dutch citizen and naturalized American named Andreas Everardus van Braam Houckgeest*, Beach Haven, NJ, 1989, 2 vols. Hendrik Doeff, *Herinneringen uit Japan*, Haarlem: F. Bohn, 1833; Hendrik Doeff, *Recollections of Japan*, trans. Annick M. Doeff, Victoria, BC: Trafford, 2003.

28. Lequin, *Isaac Titsingh*, p. 232.

29. Isaac Titsingh, *The Private Correspondence of Isaac Titsingh*, ed. Frank Lequin, Amsterdam: J. C. Gieben, 1990, vol. 1, pp. 159, 166.

30. Ibid., vol. 1, p. 73.

31. Deshima Diary, 18 September 1782, NFJ 192. Letter from Van Diemen to Van Elseracq, 2 August 1641, in VOC 865, National Archives, The Hague.

32. Leonard Blussé, "Vessel of Communication: Some Remarks about the Restricted Transfer of Maritime Know-how and Shipbuilding Technology between the Netherlands and Japan during the VOC Period," in *Transactions of the Symposium, Culture and Technology of Sea and Ship: 400 Years of History and the Next Century*, Tokyo: Japan Institute of Navigation, 1998, pp. 101–114. See also Screech, *Secret Memoirs*, pp. 46–51.

33. C. Viallé and L. Blussé, *The Deshima Dagregisters 1780–1790*, vol. 9, Leiden, 1996. p. 125. By coincidence two pictures of this vessel exist. A member of the expedition led by French discoverer Jean-François de La Pérouse made a sketch when they passed *Sankokumal* in full sea. See Screech, *Secret Memoirs*, pp. 49–50.

34. Viallé and Blussé, *The Deshima Dagregisters 1780–1790*, 25 January 1787.

35. W. J. C. Ridder Huyssen van Kattendyke, *Uittreksel uit het Dagboek, gedurende zijn verblijf in Japan in 1857, 1858, en 1859*. The Hague, 1860, pp. 219–220.

36. Edward R. Barnsley, "History of China's Retreat," paper read before the Bucks County Historical Society in Doylestown, PA, 6 May 6 1933, p. 10.

37. Simon Schama, *Patriots and Liberators: Revolution in the Netherlands, 1780–1813*, New York: Knopf, 1977; Barbara Wertheim Tuchman, *The First Salute*, New York: Knopf, 1988.

38. For a detailed study of the rape of St. Eustatius and its aftermath, see Ronald Hurst, *The Golden Rock: An episode of the American War of Independence*, Annapolis: Naval Institute Press, 1996.

39. Barnsley, *The First VBH*, vol. 1, p. 65.

40. Ibid., vol. 2, pp. 128–131.

41. Amasa Delano, *Delano's Voyages of Commerce and Discovery: Amasa Delano in China, the Pacific Islands, Australia, and South America, 1789–1807*, Stockbridge, MA: Berkshire House Publishers, 1994.

42. Louis Dermigny, *Les mémoires de Charles de Constant sur la commerce à la Chine*. Paris: SEVPEN, 1964.

43. Barnsley, *The First VBH*, vol. 1, p. 131.

44. Lequin, *Isaac Titsingh*, p. 149. For Titsingh's travel account, see Frank Lequin, *Isaac Titsingh in China (1794–1796)*, Alphen aan den Rijn: Canaletto/Repro-Holland, 2005.

45. Aeneas Anderson, *A Narrative of the British Embassy to China in the Years 1792, 1793, and 1794*, New York, 1795, pp. 222–223. J. L. Cranmer-Byng, *An Embassy to China: Lord Macartney's Journal, 1793–1794*, London: Routledge, 2000; Sir George Staunton, *An Authentic Account of an Embassy from the King of Great Britain to the Emperor of China*, Philadelphia: Printed for Robert Campbell by John Bioren, 1799, 2 vols. Sir John Barrow, *Travels in China: Containing descriptions, observations, and comparisons, made and collected in the course of a short residence at the imperial palace of Yuen-min-yuen, and on a subsequent journey through the country from Pekin to Canton . . .*, Philadelphia, 1805.

46. Hosea Ballou Morse, *The Chronicles of the East India Company trading to China 1635–1834*, Cambridge, MA, 1926, 5 vols.; Louis Dermigny, *La Chine et l'occident: Le commerce à Canton au 18e siècle, 1719–1833*, Paris: SEVPEN, 1964, 3 vols.; Michael Greenberg, *British Trade and the Opening of China 1800–1842*, Cambridge: Cambridge University Press, 1951; Earl Hampton Pritchard, *The Crucial Years of Early Anglo-Chinese Relations, 1750–1800*, Research Studies of the State College of Washington, vol. 4, nos. 3–4, Washington: Pullman, 1937.

47. Alain Peyrefitte, *The Immobile Empire*, trans. Jon Rothschild, New York: Knopf, 1992.

48. Alain Peyrefitte and Pierre Henri Durand, *Un choc de cultures: La vision des Chinois, la vision des Anglais*, Paris: Fayard, 1991, 1998, 2 vols.

49. Some very attractive essays on the significance of the Macartney embassy can be found in a small volume published on this subject: Robert A. Bickers (ed.), *Ritual and Diplomacy: The Macartney Mission to China, 1792–1794: Papers Presented at the 1992 Conference of the British Association for Chinese Studies Marking the Bicentenary of the Macartney Mission to China*, London: Wellsweep, 1993.

50. See, for instance, the heated arguments to which James Hevia's *Cherishing Men from Afar: Qing Guest Ritual and the Macartney Embassy of 1793*, Durham: Duke University Press, 1995, gave rise: Joseph W. Esherick, "Cherishing Sources from Afar"; Hevia's response, "Postpolemical Historiography"; and Esherick's final comment, "Tradutore (sic!), Traditore," *Modern China* 24, no. 2 (1998): 135–161, and no. 3 (1998): 319–327 and 328–332.

51. J. J. L. Duyvendak, "The Last Dutch Embassy to the Chinese Court," *T'oung Pao* 34, no. 4 (1938): 1–137.

52. Ibid., p. 20; Lequin, *Isaac Titsingh in China*, p. 81.

53. Imperial decree, 1 November 1794, in Fu Lo-shu, *A Documentary Chronicle of Sino-Western Relations (1644–1820)*, Tucson: University of Arizona Press, 1966, pp. 332–333.

54. Cited in Duyvendak, "The Last Dutch Embassy," p. 2.

55. Ibid., p. 3.

56. Letter from Isaac Titsingh to S. B. Nederburgh at Batavia, 26 November 1794, in Titsingh, *Private Correspondence*, vol. 1, p. 302.

57. Quoted in Geoffrey C. Ward and Frederic Delano Grant, "A Fair, Honorable, and Legitimate Trade," *American Heritage* 37, no. 5 (1986): 58.

58. Isaac Titsingh, *Mémoires et anecdotes sur la dynastie régnante des djogouns, souverains du Japon; avec la description des fêtes et ceremonies* . . . [Memoirs and Anecdotes of the Reigning Dynasty of Shoguns, Sovereigns of Japan; With a Description of the Feasts and Ceremonies], with notes and explanations by M. Abel Rémusat, Paris: A. Nepveu, 1820.

59. André Everard van Braam Houckgeest, *Voyage de l'ambassade de la Compagnie des Indes Orientales hollandaises, vers l'empereur de la Chine, dans les années 1794 & 1795* . . ., published in French by M. L. E. Moreau de Saint-Méry, Philadelphia, 1797–1798, 2 vols.

60. Eleanor H. Gustafson, "Hidden Meaning: Dutch American Andreas Everardus van Braam Houckgeest (1739–1801)," *Magazine Antiques*, October 2004.

61. Reinier H. Hesselink, "A Dutch New Year at the Shirandō Academy, 1 January 1795," *Monumenta Nipponica* 50, no. 2 (1995): 189–234.

62. Ibid., p. 218.

63. W. A. Veenhoven, *Strijd om Deshima, een onderzoek naar de aanslagen van Amerikaanse, Engelse, en Russische zijde op het Nederlandse handelsmonopolie in Japan gedurende de periode 1800–1817*, Leiden, 1950, pp. 24–31.

64. Kanai Madoka, "Salem and Nagasaki: Their Encounter 1797–1807," *Tokyo Foreign Affairs Association* (1968), reproduced from *Contemporary Japan* 29, no. 1.

65. For precise information on various partial accounts that have been published, see the introduction to Kanai Madoka (ed.), *A Diary of William Cleveland, Captain's Clerk on Board the Massachusetts*, Asian Studies Monograph Series 1, Quezon City, Philippines: Institute of Asian Studies, University of the Philippines, 1965.

66. Ibid., p. 29.

67. Ibid., pp. 31, 32.

68. Lelar's name is consistently spelled incorrectly by Lequin, who calls him Henry Zelar. For the letters of introduction and Titsingh's written advice, see Titsingh, *Private Correspondence*, vol. 2, pp. 752–758.

69. G. H. von Langsdorff, *Bemerkungen auf einer Reise um die Welt in den Jahren 1803 bis 1807*. Frankfurt am Main, 1812.

70. Keene, *Japanese Discovery*, p. 9.

71. Doeff, *Recollections of Japan*.

72. Frits Vos, "De Nederlandse taal in Japan," unpublished manuscript.

73. Doeff, *Recollections of Japan*, p. 213. Vos, "Forgotten Foibles," p. 632. The boy, who was given a position on Deshima, died of tuberculosis and melancholy at the age of seventeen.

74. Sophia Raffles, *Memoir of the life and public services of Sir Thomas Stamford Raffles*, . . . *particularly in the Government of Java, 1811–1816, and of Bencoolen and its dependencies, 1817–1824; with details of the commerce and resources of the Eastern Archipelago, and selections from his correspondence*, London, 1830.

75. Doeff, *Recollections of Japan*, p. xlii.

76. Anthony Reid and Victor Lieberman, *The Last Stand of Asian Autonomies: Responses to Modernity in the Diverse States of Southeast Asia and Korea, 1750/1900*. London: Macmillan, 1997.

77. To use Jack Wills's ringing phrase, there was a "widening stateless space" in the Eastern seas (oral communication after the Reischauer Lectures).

78. John King Fairbank, *Trade and Diplomacy on the China Coast: The Opening of the Treaty Ports 1842–1854*. Stanford: Stanford University Press, 1969.

Bibliography

Anderson, Aeneas, *A Narrative of the British Embassy to China in the Years 1792, 1793, and 1794*. New York, 1795.

Antony, Robert J., *Like Froth Floating on the Sea: The World of Pirates and Seafarers in Late Imperial South China*. Berkeley, CA: Institute of East Asian Studies, 2003.

Arasaratnam, Sinnappah, "Dutch Commercial Policy and Interests in the Malay Peninsula, 1750–1795." In Blair B. King and M. N. Pearson, eds., *The Age of Partnership, Europeans in Asia before Dominion*. Honolulu: University Press of Hawaii, 1979. Pp. 159–190.

Barnsley, Edward R., *History of China's Retreat*. Paper presented to the Bucks County Historical Society in Doylestown, PA, May 6, 1933. Reprinted for the author by the Bristol Printing Company from the *Bristol Courier* of May 9, 10, and 11, 1933.

———, *The First VBH: A biography about the remarkable life of an eighteenth-century Dutch citizen and naturalized American named Andreas Everardus van Braam Houckgeest*. Beach Haven, NJ, 1989. 2 vols.

Barrow, Sir John, *Travels in China: Containing descriptions, observations, and comparisons, made and collected in the course of a short residence at the imperial palace of Yuen-min-yuen, and on a subsequent journey through the country from Pekin to Canton* . . . Philadelphia: Printed and sold by W. F. M'Laughlin, 1805.

Basu, Dilip Kumar, *Asian Merchants and Western Trade: A Comparative Study of Calcutta and Canton, 1800–1840*. PhD dissertation, University of California, Berkeley, 1975.

———, ed., *The Rise and Growth of the Colonial Port Cities in Asia*. Lanham: University Press of America; Berkeley: Center for South and Southeast Asia Studies, University of California, 1985.

Baudet, E. H. P., *Paradise on Earth: Some Thoughts on European Images of Non-European Man*. Westport, CT: Greenwood Press, 1976.

Bell, Whitfield J., et al., *A Cabinet of Curiosities: Five Episodes in the Evolution of American Museums*. Charlottesville: University of Virginia Press, 1967.

Bentley, William, *The Diary of William Bentley, D.D., Pastor of the East Church, Sa-lem, Massachusetts (1784–December 1819)*. Salem, MA: Essex Institute, 1905; reprint, Gloucester, MA: Peter Smith, 1962. 4 vols.

Bickers, Robert A., ed., *Ritual and Diplomacy: The Macartney Mission to China, 1792–1794: Papers Presented at the 1992 Conference of the British Association for Chinese Studies Marking the Bicentenary of the Macartney Mission to China*. London: Wellsweep, 1993.

Bielenstein, Hans, *Diplomacy and Trade in the Chinese World, 589–1276*. Leiden: Brill, 2005.

Bishop, John Lyman, comp., *Studies of Governmental Institutions in Chinese History*. Cambridge, MA: Harvard University Press, 1968.

Blussé, Leonard, "Amongst Feigned Friends and Declared Enemies." In Solvi Sogner, ed., *Making Sense of Global History*. Oslo: Universitetsforlaget, 2002. Pp. 154–168.

———, *Bitter Bonds: A Colonial Divorce Drama of the Seventeenth Century*. Princeton, NJ: Markus Wiener Publishers, 2002.

———, "Brief Encounter at Macao." Special issue, *Modern Asian Studies* 22, no. 3 (1988): 647–663.

———, "Divesting a Myth: Seventeenth Century Dutch-Portuguese Rivalry in the Far East." In Anthony Disney and Emily Booth, eds., *Vasco da Gama and the Linking of Europe and Asia*. New Delhi: Oxford University Press, 2000. Pp. 387–402.

———, "No Boats to China: The Dutch East India Company and the Changing Pattern of the China Sea Trade, 1635–1690." *Modern Asian Studies* 30, no. 1 (1996): 51–76.

———, "Queen among Kings, Diplomatic Ritual at Batavia." In Kees Grijns and Peter J. M. Nas, eds., *Jakarta-Batavia*. Leiden: KITLV Press. Pp. 25–42.

———, *Strange Company: Chinese Settlers, Mestizo Women, and the Dutch in VOC Batavia*. Dordrecht, Holland: Foris Publications, 1986.

———, "Vessel of Communication: Some Remarks about the Restricted Transfer of Maritime Know-how and Shipbuilding Technology between the Nether-lands and Japan during the VOC Period." In *Transactions of the Symposium, Culture and Technology of Sea and Ship: 400 Years of History and the Next Century*. Tokyo: Japan Institute of Navigation, 1998. Pp. 101–114.

———, "The Vicissitudes of Maritime Trade: Letters from the Ocean Merchant, Li Kunhe, to the Dutch Authorities in Batavia (1803–09)." In Anthony Reid, ed., *Sojourners and Settlers: Histories of Southeast Asia and the Chinese*. St. Leo-nards, Australia: Allen and Unwin, 1996.

Blussé, Leonard, and Chen Menghong, eds., *The Archives of the Kong Koan of Bata-via*. Leiden: Brill, 2003.

Blussé, Leonard, and Femme Gaastra, *Companies and Trade: Essays on Overseas Trad-ing Companies during the Ancien Régime*. Leiden: Leiden University Press, 1981.

Blussé, Leonard, Willem Remmelink, and Ivo Smits, eds., *Bridging the Divide: 400 Years, the Netherlands–Japan*. Amsterdam: Hotei Publishing, 2000.

Blussé, Leonard, Cynthia Viallé, Willem Remmelink, and Isabel van Daalen, eds., *The Deshima Diaries: Marginalia 1740–1800*. Tokyo: Japan-Netherlands Insti-tute, 2004.

Blussé, Leonard, Wu Fengbin, Nie Dening, et al., *Gongan bu, Bacheng huaren*

Gongguan Dangan [Minutes of the Board Meetings of the Chinese Council of Batavia], Xiamen: Xiamen University Press, 2002–2007, 6 vols.

Braam Houckgeest, André Everard van, *Voyage de l'ambassade de la Compagnie des Indes Orientales hollandaises, vers l'empereur de la Chine, dans les années 1794 & 1795* [microform]: *Où se trouve la description de plusieurs parties de la Chine inconnues aux Européens, & que cette ambassade à donné l'occasion de traverser: / le tout tiré du journal d'André Everard van Braam Houckgeest, chef de la direction de la Compagnie des Indes Orientales hollandaises à la Chine, & second dans cette ambassade; ancien directeur de la Société des sciences & arts de Harlem en Hollande; de la Société philosophique de Philadelphie, &c. &c.* Published in French by M. L. E. Moreau de Saint-Méry. Philadelphia, 1797–1798. 2 vols.

Braudel, Fernand, *Civilization and Capitalism, 15th–18th Century*. New York: Harper and Row, 1982–1984. 3 vols.

Broeze, Frank, ed., *Brides of the Sea: Port Cities of Asia from the 16th–20th Centuries*. Honolulu: University of Hawaii Press, 1989.

———, ed., *Gateways of Asia: port cities of Asia in the 13th–20th centuries*. In association with the Asian Studies Association of Australia, New York: Kegan Paul International 1997.

Broeze, Frank, Peter G. Reeves, and Kenneth McPherson, eds., *Ports and Port Cities as Places of Social Interaction in the Indian Ocean Region: A Preliminary Historical Bibliography*. Perth: Centre for South and Southeast Asian Studies, University of Western Australia, 1981.

Brug, P. H. van der, *Malaria en malaise: De VOC in Batavia in de achttiende eeuw*. Amsterdam: De Bataafsche Leeuw, 1994.

Calvino, Italo, *Invisible Cities*. Translated by William Weaver. New York: Harcourt Brace Jovanovich, 1974.

Camfferman, Cees, and Terence E. Cooke, "The Profits of the Dutch East India Company's Japan Trade." *Abacus* 40, no. 1 (2004): 49–75.

Campen, Jan van, *Royers Chinese kabinet: Voorwerpen uit China verzameld door Jean Theodore Royer (1737–1807)*. Zwolle: Waanders; Amsterdam: Rijksmuseum, 2000.

———, *De Haagse jurist Jean Theodore Royer (1737–1807) en zijn verzameling Chinese voorwerpen*. Hilversum: Verloren, 2000.

Carpenter, Francis Ross, *The Old China Trade: Americans in Canton 1784–1843*. New York: Coward, McCann and Geoghegan, 1976.

Chaiklin, Martha, *Cultural Commerce and Dutch Commercial Culture: The Influence of European Material Culture on Japan, 1700–1850*. Studies in Overseas History 5, Leiden: CNWS Press, 2003.

Chang, Pin-tsun, "Chinese Maritime Trade: The Case of Sixteenth-Century Fuchien." PhD dissertation, Princeton University, 1983.———, "The First Chinese Diaspora in Southeast Asia in the Fifteenth Century." In R. Ptak and D. Rothermund, eds., *Emporia, Commodities, and Entrepreneurs in Asian Maritime Trade, c. 1400–1750*. Stuttgart: Steiner Verlag, 1991. Pp. 13–28.

———, "Maritime Trade and Local Economy in Late Ming Fukien." In E. B. Vermeer, ed., *Development and Decline of Fukien Province in the 17th and 18th Centuries*, Leiden: Brill, 1990.

Chang, Stephen Tseng-Hsin, "Commodities Imported to the Chang-chou Region of Fukian during the Late Ming Period: A Preliminary Analysis of the Tax

Lists Found in *Tung-hsi-yang k'ao'*." In R. Ptak and D. Rothermund, eds., *Emporia, Commodities, and Entrepreneurs in Asian Maritime Trade, c. 1400–1750*. Stuttgart: Steiner Verlag, 1991. Pp. 159–194.

Chaudhuri, K. N., *The Trading World of Asia and the English East India Company, 1660–1760*. Cambridge: Cambridge University Press, 1978.

Ch'en Kuo-tung, Anthony, *The Insolvency of the Chinese Hong Merchants, 1760–1843*. Institute of Economics Academia Sinica, Monograph Series no. 45. Nankang, Taiwan: Institute of Economics, Academia Sinica, 1990.

Chen, Xiyu, *Zhongguo fanchuan yu haiwai maoyi* [Chinese Sailing Ships and Overseas Trade], Xiamen: n.p., 1991.

Cheong, Weng Eang, *Hong Merchants of Canton: Chinese Merchants in Sino-Western Trade 1684–1768*. Richmond, Surrey: Curzon Press, 1997.

Chijs, J. A. van der, *Nederlandsch-Indisch Plakaatboek 1602–1811*. Batavia: Landsdrukkerij, 1885–1900. 17 vols.

Chin, James K., "Merchants and Other Sojourners: The Hokkien Overseas, 1570–1760." PhD dissertation, University of Hong Kong, 1998.

Cleveland, Richard J., *A Narrative of Voyages and Commercial Enterprises, by Richard J. Cleveland (1773–1860)*. Boston: C. H. Peirce, 1850.

Constant, Charles Samuel de, *Les mémoires de Charles de Constant sur le commerce à la Chine*. Edited by Louis Dermigny. Paris: SEVPEN, 1964.

Cranmer-Byng, J. L., *An Embassy to China: Lord Macartney's Journal, 1793–1794*. London: Routledge, 2000.

Crossman, Carl L., *The China Trade: Export Paintings, Furniture, Silver & Other Objects*. Princeton, NJ: Pyne Press, 1972.

Cushman, Jennifer W., *Fields from the Sea: Chinese Junk Trade with Siam during the Late Eighteenth and Early Nineteenth Centuries*, Ithaca: Cornell University Press, 1975.

Delano, Amasa, *Delano's Voyages of Commerce and Discovery: Amasa Delano in China, the Pacific Islands, Australia, and South America, 1789–1807*. Edited and with an introduction by Eleanor Roosevelt Seagraves. Foreword by William T. LaMoy. Stockbridge, MA: Berkshire House Publishers, 1994. [Original title: *A Narrative of Voyages and Travels in the Northern and Southern Hemispheres*.]

Dennett, Tyler, *Americans in Eastern Asia: A Critical Study of the Policy of the United States with Reference to China, Japan, and Korea in the 19th Century*. New York: Octagon Books, 1979.

Dennys, N. B., ed., *The Treaty Ports of China and Japan: A Complete Guide to the Open Ports of Those Countries, Together with Peking, Yedo, Hongkong and Macao. Forming a guide book & vademecum for travellers, merchants, and residents in general*. By Wm. Fred. Mayers, N. B. Dennys, and Chas. King. London: Trübner and Co., 1867.

Dermigny, Louis, *La Chine et l'occident: Le commerce à Canton au 18e siècle, 1719–1833*. Paris: SEVPEN, 1964. 3 vols.

———, *Les mémoires de Charles de Constant sur la commerce à la Chine*. Paris: SEVPEN, 1964.

Dillo, Ingrid G., *De nadagen van de Verenigde Oostindische Compagnie, 1783–1795: Schepen en zeevarenden*. Amsterdam: De Bataafsche Leeuw, 1992.

Dirks, Nicholas B., *The Scandal of Empire: India and the Creation of Imperial Britain*. Cambridge, MA: Belknap Press of Harvard University Press, 2006.

Doeff, Hendrik, *Herinneringen uit Japan*. Haarlem: F. Bohn, 1833.

———, *Recollections of Japan*. Translated and annotated by Annick M. Doeff. Victoria, BC: Trafford, 2003.

Downs, Jacques M., *The Golden Ghetto: The American Commercial Community at Canton and the Shaping of American China Policy, 1784–1844*. Bethlehem, PA: Lehigh University Press, 1997.

Dulles, Foster Rhea, *The Old China Trade*. Boston: Houghton Mifflin Company, 1930.

Duyvendak, J. J. L., "The Last Dutch Embassy to the Chinese Court." *T'oung Pao* 34, no. 4 (1938): 1–137.

Earl, George Windsor, *The Eastern Seas or Voyages and Adventures in the Indian Archipelago in 1832–33–34, comprising a tour of the island of Java-visits to Borneo, the Malay peninsula, Siam etc; also an account of the present state of Singapore with observations on the commercial resources of the archipelago*. London: W. Allen and Co., 1837.

Eyck van Heslinga, E. S. van, *Van compagnie naar koopvaardij: De scheepvaartverbinding van de Bataafse Republiek met de koloniën in Azië 1795–1806*. Amsterdam: Bataafsche Leeuw, 1988.

Fairbank, John King, *Trade and Diplomacy on the China Coast: The Opening of the Treaty Ports 1842–1854*. Stanford: Stanford University Press, 1969.

Fairbank, John King, ed., *The Chinese World Order: Traditional China's Foreign Relations*. Cambridge, MA: Harvard University Press, 1968.

Fairbank, John King, Edwin Reischauer, and Albert M. Craig, *East Asia: The Modern Transformation*. Boston: Houghton Mifflin, 1965.

Feenstra Kuiper, Jan, *Japan en de buitenwereld in de achttiende eeuw*. The Hague: M. Nijhoff, 1921.

Feldbæk, Ole, *India Trade under the Danish Flag 1772–1808: European Enterprise and Anglo-Indian Remittance and Trade*. Lund: Studentlitteratur, 1969.

Fichter, James, "American East Indies, 1773–1815." PhD dissertation, Harvard University, 2006.

Forbes, R. B., *Remarks on China and the China Trade*. Boston: Samuel N. Dickinson, printer, 1844.

Frankel, Jeffrey, "The 1807–1809 Embargo against Great Britain." *Journal of Economic History* 17, no. 2 (1982): 296–308.

French, Calvin L., *Shiba Kōkan: Artist, Innovator, and Pioneer in the Westernization of Japan*. New York: Weatherhill, 1966.

Fu, Lo-shu, *A Documentary Chronicle of Sino-Western Relations (1644–1820)*. Tucson: University of Arizona Press, 1966. 2 vols.

Gaastra, Femme S., *The Dutch East India Company: Expansion and Decline*. Zutphen: De Walburg Pers, 2003.

Gobel, Erik, "The Danish Asiatic Company's Voyages to China 1732–1833." *Scandinavian Economic History Review* 27, no. 1 (1979): 1–25.

Goldstein, Jonathan, *Philadelphia and the China Trade 1682–1846, Commercial, Cultural and Attitudinal Effects*. University Park: Pennsylvania State University Press, 1978.

Golovnin, Vasilii Mikhailovich, *Narrative of my captivity in Japan, during the years 1811, 1812 & amp; 1813, by Captain Golownin, R.N. To which is added an account of voyages to the coasts of Japan, and of negotiations with the Japanese, for the release of the author and his companions, by Captain Rikord*. London: Printed for H. Colburn, 1818. 2 vols.

Goodman, Grant Kohn, *Japan and the Dutch, 1600–1853*. Richmond, Surrey: Curzon Press, 2000.

Goodrich, Carter, comp., *The Government and the Economy, 1783–1861*. Indianapolis: Bobbs-Merrill, 1967.

Grant, Frederic Delano, "Hong Merchant Litigation in the American Courts." In *Proceedings of the Massachusetts Historical Society*, vol. 99 (1987). Boston: Northeastern University Press, 1988. Pp. 44–62.

———, "Merchants, Lawyers, and the China Trade of Boston." *Boston Bar Journal* 23, no. 8 (September 1979): 5–16.

———, "The Present Relevance of Historical American Trade with China." Paper delivered at symposium The New England China Trade—Then and Now, Boston Athenaeum, Boston, May 20, 2005.

Greenberg, Michael, *British Trade and the Opening of China 1800–1842*. Cambridge: Cambridge University Press, 1951.

Groot, Henk de, "The Study of the Dutch Language in Japan during Its Period of National Isolation (ca. 1641–1868)." Dissertation, University of Canterbury, New Zealand, 2007.

Guignes, Chrétien-Louis-Joseph de, *Voyages à Peking, Manille et l'île de France, faits dans l'intervalle des années 1784 à 1801*. Paris: Imprimerie impériale, 1808. 3 vols.

Gunn, Geoffrey C., *Nagasaki in the Asian Bullion Trade Networks*. Tonan Ajiakenkyu sosho 32. Nagasaki: Nagasaki daigaku keizaibu Tonan-ajia kenkyujo, 1999.

Haan, Frederik de, *Oud Batavia*. Bandung: A. C. Nix, 1935. 2 vols.

Haga, Tōru, *Sugita Genpaku, Hiraga Gennai, Shiba Kōkan*. Tokyo: Chūō Kōronsha, 1971.

Hamashita, Takeshi, "The Intra-regional System in East Asia in Modern Times." In Peter J. Katzenstein and Takashi Shiraishi, eds., *Network Power: Japan and Asia*. Ithaca: Cornell University Press, 1997.

———, *Kindai chūgoku no kokusaiteki keiki: chōkō bōeki shisutemu to kindai Ajia:* [Early Modern China's International Turning Points: The Tribute Trade System and Early Modern Asia]. Tokyo: Tōkyō Daigaku Shuppankai, 1990.

Heath, Peter, "War and Peace in the Works of Erasmus: A Medieval Perspective." In Andrew Ayton and J. L. Price, eds., *The Medieval Military Revolution: State, Society and Military Change in Medieval and Early Modern Europe*. London: I. B. Taurus Publishers, 1995. Pp. 121–144.

Heek, Frederik van, *Chineesche Immigranten in Nederland*. Amsterdam: J. Emmering, 1936.

Hesselink, Reinier H., "A Dutch New year at the Shirandô Academy, 1 January 1795." *Monumenta Nipponica* 50, no. 2 (1995): 189–234.

Hevia, James Louis, *Cherishing Men from Afar: Qing Guest Ritual and the Macartney Embassy of 1793*. Durham: Duke University Press, 1995.

Hickey, William, *Memoirs of William Hickey*. Edited by Peter Quennell. London: Routledge and Kegan Paul, 1975.

Historiographical Institute, ed., *Oranda Shôkancho Nikki: Diaries Kept by the Heads of the Dutch Factory in Japan 1633–1647* [Original Dutch Texts]. Tokyo: Historiographical Institute, 1974–2003, 10 vols.; Japanese translation, 1976–2004, 10 vols.

Hoang, Anh Tuan, *Silk for Silver: Dutch-Vietnamese Relations, 1637–1700,* TANAP Monographs on the History of Asian-European Interaction 5. Leiden: Brill, 2007.

Hobhouse, Henry, *Seeds of Wealth: Four Plants That Made Men Rich.* London: Macmillan, 2003.

Hostetler, Laura, *Qing Colonial Enterprise, Ethnography and Cartography in Early Modern China.* Chicago: University of Chicago Press, 2001.

Howard, David Sanctuary, *New York and the China Trade.* With an essay by Conrad Edick Wright. New York: New York Historical Society, 1984.

———, *A Tale of Three Cities: Canton, Shanghai and Hong Kong: Three Centuries of Sino-British Trade in the Decorative Arts.* London: Sotheby's, 1997.

Hullu, J. de, "A. E. Van Braam Houckgeest's memorie over Malakka en den tinhandel aldaar (1790)." *Bijdragen tot de Taal-, Land- en Volkenkunde van Nederlandsch-Indië,* KITLV, 76 (1920): 284–309.

———, "De instelling van de commissie voor den handel der Oost-Indische Compagnie op China in 1756" [The Establishment of the Committee for the China Trade of the East India Company in 1756], *Bijdragen tot de Taal-, Land-, en Volkenkunde van Nederlandsch-Indië,* KITLV, (1923): 529–533.

———, "On the Rise of the Indies Trade of the United States of America as Competitor of the East India Company in the Period 1786–1790." In M. A. P. Meilink-Roelofsz, ed., *Dutch Authors on Asian History.* Dordrecht: Foris Publications, 1988. Pp. 138–154.

Hurst, Ronald, *The Golden Rock: An Episode of the American War of Independence.* Annapolis: Naval Institute Press, 1996.

Huyssen van Kattendyke, W. J. C. Ridder, *Uittreksel uit het Dagboek, gedurende zijn verblijf in Japan in 1857, 1858, en 1859.* The Hague, 1860.

Ideal Commonwealths: Comprising, More's Utopia, Bacon's New Atlantis, Campanella's City of the Sun, and Harriton's Oceana, Introduction by Henry Morley. P. F. Collier and Son; New York: The Colonial Press, 1914.

Idema, Wilt, "Vreemde bedden en een grabbelton." *Armada* 19 (2000): 25–29.

Irick, Robert L., *Ch'ing Policy toward the Coolie Trade 1847–1878.* Taipei: CMC Publishing, 1982.

Irwin, Douglas A., "The Welfare Cost of Autarky: Evidence from the Jeffersonian Trade Embargo, 1807–09." *Review of International Economics* 13, no. 4 (2005): 631–645.

Iwao, Seiichi, et al., eds., *Oranda fūsetsugaki shūsei* [A Compilation of the Dutch News], Nichi-Ran Gakkai, Hōsei Rangaku Kenkyūkai hen. Tokyo: Yoshikawa Kōbunkan, 1977–1979. 2 vols.

Jansen, Marius B., "Rangaku and Westernization." *Modern Asian Studies* 18, no. 4 (1984): 542.

Kaempfer, Engelbert, *The Furthest Goal: Engelbert Kaempfer's Encounter with Tokugawa Japan.* Edited by Beatrice M. Bodart-Bailey and Derek Massarella. Folkestone, Kent: Japan Library, 1995.

———, *The History of Japan.* Reprint; Richmond, Surrey: Curzon Press, 1993.

Kanai, Madoka, ed., *A Diary of William Cleveland, Captain's Clerk on Board the Massachusetts.* Asian Studies, Monograph Series 1. Quezon City: Institute of Asian Studies, University of the Philippines, 1965.

———, "Salem and Nagasaki: Their Encounter 1797–1807." In *Tokyo Foreign Affairs Association* (1968). Reproduced from *Contemporary Japan* 29, no. 1.

Keene, Donald, *The Japanese Discovery of Europe, 1720–1830*. Revised edition. Stanford: Stanford University Press, 1969.

———, *Travelers of a Hundred Ages*. New York: H. Holt and Co., 1989.

Kent, Henry W., "Van Braam Houckgeest, an Early American Collector." *Proceedings of the American Antiquarian Society* 40, new series (October 1930): 159–174.

Kling, Blair B., and M. N. Pearson, eds., *The Age of Partnership: Europeans in Asia before Dominion*. Honolulu: University Press of Hawaii, 1979.

Kroeskamp, H., "De Chinezen te Batavia (1700) als exempel voor de Christenen van West Europa." *Indonesië* 6, no. 4 (1953): 346–371.

Kuhn, Philip A., *Origins of the Modern Chinese State*. Stanford: Stanford University Press, 2002.

Kuwabara, Jitsuzo, "On P'u Shou-keng." *Memoirs of the Research Department of the Toyo Bunko* 2 (1928): 1–79; 7 (1935): 1–104.

Langsdorff, G. H. von, *Bemerkungen auf einer Reise um die Welt in den Jahren 1803 bis 1807*. Frankfurt am Main, 1812.

Latourette, Kenneth Scott, *Voyages of American Ships to China, 1784–1844*. New Haven: Connecticut Academy of Arts and Sciences, 1927.

———, *The History of Early Relations between the United States and China, 1784–1844*. New Haven: Yale University Press, 1917.

Leonard, Jane Kate, *Wei Yuan and China's Rediscovery of the Maritime World*. Cambridge, MA: Council on East Asian Studies, Harvard University, distributed by Harvard University Press, 1984.

Lee, Jean Gordon, *Philadelphians and the China Trade, 1784–1844*. With an essay by Philip Chadwick Foster Smith. Philadelphia: Philadelphia Museum of Art, 1984.

Lequin, Frank, *Isaac Titsingh (1745–1812), een passie voor Japan. Leven en werk van de grondlegger van de Europese Japanologie*. Alphen aan den Rijn: Canaletto/Repro-Holland, 2002.

———, *Isaac Titsingh in China (1794–1796)*. Alphen aan den Rijn: Canaletto/Repro-Holland, 2005.

Liang, Jiabin, *Guangdong shi san hang kao* [A Study of the Thirteen "Hong"]. Guangzhou: Guangdong renmin chuban she, 1999.

Liao, Dage, *Fujian haiwai jiaotongshi* [A General History of the Maritime Trade of Fujian]. Fuzhou: Fujian renmin chubanshe, 2002.

Lin, Renchuan, *Fujian dui haiwai maoyi yu haiguanshi* [The History of Fujian's Overseas Trade and the Customs]. Xiamen: Lujiang chubanshe, 1991.

Liu, Yong, *The Dutch East India Company's Tea Trade with China, 1757–1781*. TANAP Monographs on the History of Asian-European Interaction 6. Leiden: Brill, 2007.

Ljungstedt, Anders, *An Historical Sketch of the Portuguese Settlements in China, and of the Roman Catholic Church and Mission in China; A Supplementary Chapter, Description of the City of Canton*. Hong Kong: Viking Publications, 1992.

Loehr, George, "A. E. van Braam Houckgeest, the First American at the Court of China." *Princeton University Library Chronicle* 15, no. 4 (1954): 179–193; http://libweb5.princeton.edu/visual_materials/pulc/pulc_v_15_n_4.pdf.

Loos-Haaxman, J. de, *Johannes Rach en zijn werk*. De topografische beschrijving der teekeningen met medewerking van W. Fruin-Mees door P. C. Bloys van Treslong Prins. Batavia: G. Kolff and Co., 1928.

Macartney, George, *An Embassy to China: Being the Journal Kept by Lord Macartney during His Embassy to the Emperor Ch'ien-lung, 1793–1794.* Edited with an introduction and notes by J. L. Cranmer-Byng. London: Longmans, 1972.

Matsukata, Fuyuko, *Oranda Fusetsugaki to Kinsei Nihon* [The Dutch World News and Early Modern Japan]. Tokyo: Tokyo University Press, 2007.

———, "1660-nendai fusetsugaki no kakuritsu katei" [The Formalization Process of Fusetsugaki in the 1660s], in Fujita Satoru, ed., *17-seiki no Nihon to Higashi Ajia.* Tokyo, 2000.

McPherson, Kenneth, "Port Cities as Nodal Points of Change: The Indian Ocean, 1890s–1920s." In Leila Tarazi Fawaz and C. A. Bayly, eds., *Modernity and Culture: From the Mediterranean to the Indian Ocean.* New York: Columbia University Press, 2002.

Meilink-Roelofsz, M. A. P., "Ulrich Gualtherus Hemmingson, V.O.C. dienaar en verbindingsschakel tussen China en Nederland." *Nederlands Kunsthistorisch Jaarboek,* 31 (1980): 456–474.

Meilink-Roelofsz, M. A. P., R. Raben, and H. Spijkerman, eds., *De archieven van de Verenigde Oostindische Compagnie/The archives of the Dutch East India Company (1602–1795), History and Manual.* The Hague: Sdu Uitgeverij, 1992.

Meylan, Germain Felix, *Japan: Voorgesteld in schetsen over de zeden en gebruiken van dat ryk, byzonder over de ingezetenen der stad Nagasaky.* Amsterdam: M. Westerman and Zoon, 1830.

Milburn, William, *Oriental Commerce: Containing a Geographical Description of the Principal Places in the East Indies, China, and Japan, With Their Produce, Manufactures, and Trade.* London: Black, Parry and Co., 1813.

More, Sir Thomas, *Utopia (De optimo reip. statv, deqve noua insula Vtopia).* Translated by Robert Adams. New York: W. W. Norton, 1991.

Moreau de Saint-Méry, M. L. E., *Moreau de St. Méry's American Journey 1793–1798.* Translated and edited by Kenneth Roberts [and] Anna M. Roberts. Preface by Kenneth Roberts. Introduction by Stewart L. Mims. Garden City, NY: Doubleday, 1947.

Morrison, John Robert, *A Chinese Commercial Guide: Consisting of a Collection of Details and Regulations Respecting Foreign Trade with China.* Third edition. Revised throughout and made applicable to the trade as at present conducted. Canton: Office of the Chinese Repository, 1848.

Morse, Hosea Ballou, *The Chronicles of the East India Company Trading to China 1635–1834.* Cambridge, MA, 1926. 5 vols.

Müller, Klaus, "Shiba Kokan und sein Seiyo-gadan als Beispiel für die Entstehung kunstfremder Einflüsse in der westlichen Malerei der Edo-Zeit." In Lydia Brüll and Ulrich Kemper eds., *Asien, Tradition und Fortschritt: Festschrift für Horst Hammitzsch zu seinem 60. Geburtstag.* Wiesbaden: O. Harrassowitz, 1971. Pp. 416–431.

Murphey, Roads, "Traditionalism and Colonialism: Changing Urban Roles in Asia." *Journal of Asian Studies* 29 (1969): 83.

Murray, Dian, "Conflict and Coexistence: The Sino-Vietnamese Maritime Boundaries in Historical Perspective." Center for Southeast Asian Studies, Occasional Papers no. 13, University of Wisconsin, Madison, 1988.

———, *Pirates of the South China Coast, 1790–1810.* Stanford: Stanford University Press, 1987.

Nagasaki City Government, ed., *Nagasaki shishi* [A History of Nagasaki]. Nagasaki: Nagasaki Shiyakusho, 1923–1935. 8 vols.

Nagazumi, Yoko, "Eighteenth and Early Nineteenth Centuries Progress of the Competence in Dutch and the Russian Problem in Japan." *The Toyo Gakuho* 78, no. 4 (1997): 10–30.

———, "The Decline of Trade and Russian Expansion in East Asia." In Leonard Blussé, Willem Remmelink, and Ivo Smits, eds., *Bridging the Divide: 400 Years, the Netherlands-Japan*. Amsterdam: Hotei Publishing, 2000. Pp. 55–72.

Niemeijer, Hendrik E., *Batavia: een koloniale samenleving in de zeventiende eeuw*. Amsterdam: Balans, 2005.

Ng, Chin-Keong, *Trade and Society: The Amoy Network on the China Coast, 1683–1735*. Singapore: Singapore University Press, 1983.

Ong-Dae-Hae, *The Chinaman Abroad: or a Desultory Account of the Malayan Archipelago, Particularly of Java*. Translated by W. H. Medhurst. Shanghai, 1848.

Oosterhoff, J. L., "Zeelandia: A Dutch Colonial City on Formosa (1624–1662)." In Robert Ross and Gerard Telkamp, eds., *Colonial Cities*. Dordrecht: Martinus Nijhoff, 1985. Pp. 51–64.

Peabody Museum of Salem, *Portraits of Shipmasters and Merchants in the Peabody Museum of Salem*. Introduction by Walter Muir Whitehill. Salem: Newcomb and Gauss Co., 1939.

Peyrefitte, Alain, *The Immobile Empire*. Translated by Jon Rothschild. New York: Knopf, 1992.

Peyrefitte, Alain, and Pierre Henri Durand, *Un choc de cultures: La vision des Chinois, la vision des Anglais*. Paris: Fayard 1991, 1998. 2 vols.

Pritchard, Earl Hampton, *The Crucial Years of Early Anglo-Chinese Relations, 1750–1800*. Research Studies of the State College of Washington, vol. 4, nos. 3–4. Washington: Pullman, 1937.

Ptak, Roderich, and Dietmar Rothermund, eds., *Emporia, Commodities, and Entrepreneurs in Asian Maritime Trade, c. 1400–1750*. Stuttgart: Steiner Verlag, 1991.

Raben, Remco, "Round about Batavia: Ethnicity and Authority in the Ommelanden, 1650–1800." In K. Grijns and Peter J. M. Nas, eds., *Jakarta-Batavia. Socio-cultural Essays*. Leiden: KITLV Press, 2000. Pp. 93–113.

Raffles, Sophia, *Memoir of the life and public services of Sir Thomas Stamford Raffles, . . . particularly in the Government of Java, 1811–1816, and of Bencoolen and its dependencies, 1817–1824; with details of the commerce and resources of the Eastern Archipelago, and selections from his correspondence*. London, 1830.

Reeves, Peter G., *Ports and Port Cities as Places of Social Interaction in the Indian Ocean Region: A Preliminary Historical Bibliography*, Perth: Centre for South and Southeast Asian Studies, University of Western Australia, 1981.

Reid, Anthony (and Victor Lieberman), *The Last Stand of Asian Autonomies: Responses to Modernity in the Diverse States of Southeast Asia and Korea, 1750/1900*. London: Macmillan, 1997.

Reischauer, Edwin, *Ennin's Travels in T'ang China*. New York: Ronald Press Company, 1955.

Reischauer, Edwin O., and John King Fairbank, *East Asia: The Great Tradition*. Boston: Houghton Mifflin, 1960.

Rekishigaku Kenkyukai [Historical Research Society], ed., *Minatomachi no sekkaishi* [Port Cities in World History]. Tokyo: Aoki Shoten Publishing, 2005. 3 vols.

Rowe, William T. *Saving the World: Chen Hongmou and Elite Consciousness in Eighteenth-Century China*. Stanford: Stanford University Press, 2001.

Ruangsilp, Bhawan, *Dutch East India Company Merchants at the Court of Ayutthaya: Dutch Perceptions of the Thai Kingdom, c. 1604–1765.* TANAP Monographs on the History of Asian-European Interaction 8. Leiden: Brill, 2007.

Saitō, Agu, *Zūfu to Nihon* [Doeff and Japan]. Tokyo: Kōbunkan, 1922.

Sakamaki, Shunzo, "Japan and the United States, 1790–1853." *Transactions of the Asiatic Society of Japan*, vol. 18. Tokyo, 1939.

Schama, Simon, *Patriots and Liberators: Revolution in the Netherlands, 1780–1813.* New York: Knopf, 1977.

Schottenhammer, Angela, ed., *Trade and Transfer across the East Asian "Mediterranean."* Wiesbaden: Harrassowitz, 2005.

Schottenhammer, Angela, and Roderich Ptak, eds., *The Perception of Maritime Space in Traditional Chinese Sources*, East Asian Maritime History 2. Wiesbaden: Harassowitz, 2006.

Screech, Timon, *Japan Extolled and Decried: Carl Peter Thunberg and the Shogun's Realm, 1775–1796.* Annotated and introduced by Timon Screech. New York: Routledge, 2005.

———, *The Lens within the Heart: The Western Scientific Gaze and Popular Imagery in Later Edo Japan.* Honolulu: University of Hawai'i Press, 2002.

———, *Secret Memoirs of the Shoguns: Isaac Titsingh and Japan, 1779–1822.* Annotated and introduced by Timon Screech. London; New York: Routledge, 2006.

Shaw, Samuel, *The Journals of Major Samuel Shaw: The First American Consul at Canton. With a Life of the Author by Josiah Quincy.* Boston: Wm. Crosby and H. P. Nichols, 1847.

Shiba, Kōkan, *Edo, Nagasaki e kikō: saiyū ryodan* [Edo, Nagasaki, Illustrated Account of a Western Journey]. Tokyo: Kokusho Kankōkai, 1992.

———, *Kōkan saiyū nikki* [The Diary of Kokan's Western Journey]. Edited by Haga Tōru and Ōta Rieko. Tokyo: Heibonsha, 1986.

Shimada, Ryuto, *The Intra-Asian Trade in Japanese Copper by the Dutch East India Company during the Eighteenth Century.* TANAP Monographs on the History of the Asian-European Interaction 4. Leiden: Brill, 2006.

Singh, S. B., *European Agency Houses in Bengal (1783–1833).* Calcutta: Firma K. L. Mukhopadhyay, 1966.

So, Billy K. L., *Prosperity, Region, and Institutions in Maritime China: The South Fukien Pattern, 946–1368.* Cambridge, MA: Harvard University Press, 2000.

Spence, Jonathan D., and John E. Wills, eds., *From Ming to Ch'ing: Conquest, Region, and Continuity in Seventeenth-Century China.* New Haven: Yale University Press, 1979.

Staunton, Sir George, *An Authentic Account of an Embassy from the King of Great Britain to the Emperor of China.* Philadelphia: Printed for Robert Campbell by John Bioren, 1799. 2 vols.

Steensgaard, Niels, "The Dutch East India Company as an Institutional Innovation." In Maurice Aymar, ed., *Dutch Capitalism and World Capitalism.* New York: Cambridge University Press, 1977. Pp. 235–258.

———, "Emporia: Some Reflections." in R. Ptak and D. Rothermund, eds., *Emporia, Commodities, and Entrepreneurs in Asian Maritime Trade, c. 1400–1750.* Stuttgart: Steiner Verlag, 1991. Pp. 13–28.

Struve, Lynn A., ed., *The Qing Formation in World-Historical Time.* Cambridge, MA: Harvard University Press, 2004.

Sung An-yun, "A Study of the Thirteen Hongs of Kuangtung: A Translation of Parts of the Kuangtung Shih-San-Hang Kao of Liang Chia-pin." MA thesis, Department of History, University of Chicago, 1958.

Tabohashi, Kiyoshi, *Zōtei Kindai Nihon gaikoku kankeishi* [Japan's Foreign Relations in Early Modern Time]. Expanded edition. Tokyo: Hara Shobō, 1976.

Tian, Rukang, *Zhongguo fan chuan mao yi he dui wai guanxi shi lun ji* [A Collection of Historical Essays on the Trade of Chinese Sailing Ships and Foreign Relations]. Hangzhou: Zhejiang renmin chuban she, 1987.

T'ien, Ju-k'ang, "The Chinese Junk Trade: Merchants, Entrepreneurs, and Coolies, 1600–1850." In Klaus Friedland, ed., *Maritime Aspects of Migration*. Cologne: Böhlau, 1987. Pp. 381–389.

Titsingh, Isaac, *Mémoires et anecdotes sur la dynastie régnante des djogouns, souverains du Japon; avec la description des fêtes et cérémonies . . .* With notes and explanations by M. Abel Rémusat. Paris: A. Nepveu, 1820.

———, *The Private Correspondence of Isaac Titsingh*. Edited by Frank Lequin. Amsterdam: J. C. Gieben, 1990. 2 vols.

Torbert, Preston M., *The Ch'ing Imperial Household Department: A Study of Its Organization and Principal Functions, 1662–1796*. Cambridge, MA: Harvard University Press, 1977.

Trocki, Carl, "Chinese Pioneering in Eighteenth-Century Southeast Asia." In Anthony Reid, ed., *The Last Stand of Asian Autonomies*. New York: Macmillan, 1997. Pp. 83–101.

Tsūkō ichiran [A Synopsis of Navigations]. Edited by Hayashi Fukusai. Tokyo: Kokusho Kankōkai, 1912–1913. 8 vols.

Tsūkō ichiran: zokushū (A Synopsis of Navigations: Supplement]. Edited by Yanai Kenji. Osaka: Seibundō, Shōwa 43–48 [i.e. 1968–1973]. 5 vols.

Tuchman, Barbara Wertheim, *The First Salute*. New York: Knopf, 1988.

Tuck, Patrick, ed., *Britain and the China Trade 1635–1842*. London: Routledge, 2000. 10 vols.

Valentijn, F., *Oud en Nieuw Oost-Indiën* [Old and New East Indies]. Dordrecht: J. van Braam, 1724–1726. 5 vols. in 8.

Van Dyke, Paul A., *The Canton Trade: Life and Enterprise on the China Coast 1700–1845*. Hong Kong: Hongkong University Press, 2005.

———, "The Yan family, Merchants of Canton 1734–1780s." *Revista de Cultura*, International Edition 9 (January 2005): 30–85.

Veenhoven, W. A., *Strijd om Deshima, een onderzoek naar de aanslagen van Amerikaanse, Engelse, en Russische zijde op het Nederlandse handelsmonopolie in Japan gedurende de periode 1800–1817*. Doctoral thesis. Leiden, 1950.

Velde, Paul van der, and Rudolf Bachofner, *The Deshima Diaries Marginalia 1700–1740*. Tokyo: Japan-Netherlands Institute, 1992.

Viallé, Cynthia, "In Aid of Trade: Dutch Gift-Giving in Tokugawa Japan." *Tokyo Daigaku shiryohensanjo kenkyu kiyo* 16 (2006): 57–78.

Viallé, Cynthia, and Leonard Blussé, *The Deshima Dagregisters 1640–1660*, Intercontinenta Series nos. 23, 25. Leiden: IGEER, 2001, 2005, 2 vols.

Viraphol, Sarasin, *Tribute and Profit: Sino-Siamese Trade, 1652–1853*. Cambridge, MA: Harvard University Press, 1977.

Vos, Frits, "De Nederlandse taal in Japan." Unpublished manuscript.

———, "Forgotten Foibles: Love and the Dutch on Deshima." In Lydia Brüll und Ulrich Kemper, eds., *Asien, Tradition und Fortschritt; Festschrift für Horst*

Hammitzsch zu seinem 60. Geburtstag. Wiesbaden: O. Harrassowitz, 1971. Pp. 614–633.

Ward, Geoffrey C., and Frederic Delano Grant, "A Fair, Honorable, and Legitimate Trade." *American Heritage* 37, no. 5 (1986): 49–65.

Warren, James Francis, *The Global Economy and the Sulu Zone: Connections, Commodities, and Culture.* Quezon City, Philippines: New Day Publishers, 2000.

———, *Iranun and Balaningi: Globalization, Maritime Raiding and the Birth of Ethnicity.* Kent Ridge, Singapore: Singapore University Press, 2002.

———, *The Sulu Zone, 1768–1898: The Dynamics of External Trade, Slavery, and Ethnicity in the Transformation of a Southeast Asian Maritime State.* Kent Ridge, Singapore: Singapore University Press, 1981.

Wells Williams, S., *The Chinese Commercial Guide, containing treaties, tariffs, regulations, tables, etc., useful in the trade to China & Eastern Asia with an appendix of sailing directions for those seas and coasts.* Taipei: Ch'eng-wen Publishing Company, 1966.

Wiethoff, Bodo. *Die chinesische Seeverbotspolitik und der private Überseehandel von 1368 bis 1567.* Hamburg: Gesellschaft für Natur- und Völkerkunde Ostasiens, 1963.

Whitehill, Walter Muir, *The East India Marine Society and the Peabody Museum of Salem: A Sesquicentennial History.* Salem, MA: Peabody Museum, 1949.

Wills, John E., *Pepper, Guns, and Parleys: The Dutch East India Company and China, 1662–1681,* Cambridge, MA: Harvard University Press, 1974.

Wills, J. E., "Qing Relations with Annam and Siam, 1680–1810." Paper presented at the Eighteenth IAHA Conference, Taipei, December 2004.

Wong, R. Bin, "The Search for European Differences and Domination in the Early Modern World: A View from Asia." *American Historical Review* 107, no. 2 (2002).

Xiang, Da, *Liang zhong hai dao zhen jing* [Two Maritime Itineraries]. Beijing: Zhonghua shu ju, 1961.

Xie, Qinggao (as told by), *Hai lu jiao shi* [Discourse on the Sea]. Noted down by Yang Bingnan. Annotated by An Jing. Beijing: Shangwu yinshuguan, 2002.

Yamawaki, Teijirō, *Nagasaki no Oranda shōkan: Sekai no naka no sakoku Nihon* [The Dutch Trading Factory at Nagasaki: The Seclusion of Japan within the World]. Tokyo: Chūō Kōronsha, 1980.

———, *Nagasaki no Tōjin bōeki* [The Trade of the Chinese at Nagasaki]. Tokyo: Yoshikawa Kōbunkan, 1964.

Yin, Kuang-jen, *Ou-Mun Kei Leok (Monografia de Macau)* por Tcheong-Ü-Lâm e Ian-Kuong-Iâm. Translated from Chinese into Portuguese by Luís G. Gomes. Macau: Editada pela Repartição Central dos Serviços Económicos, Secção de Publicidade e Turismo, Quinzena de Macau, 1979.

Yuan, Bingling, *Chinese Democracies, a Study of the Kongsis of West Borneo (1776–1884).* CNWS Publications 79. Leiden: Research School CNWS, Leiden University, 2000, pp. 302–303.

Yung, Lun yuen, *History of the Pirates Who Infested the China Sea from 1807 to 1810.* Translated with notes and illustrations by Charles Fried. London: Neumann, 1831.

Zhang, Xie, *Dong xi yang kao* [A Treatise on the Eastern and Western Oceans]. Beijing: Zhonghua shuju, 1981.

Zhao, Gang, "Reshaping the Asian Trade Network: The Construction and Exe-

cution of the 1684 Chinese Open Trade Policies." PhD dissertation, Johns
    Hopkins University, 2006.
Zhu, Yong, *Bu yuan da kai di Zhongguo da men: 18 shiji di wai xiao yu Zhongguo ming
    yun* [The Gate of China That Was Not Opened: Eighteenth-Century Foreign
    Relations and China's Fate]. Nanchang: Jiangxi renmin chuban she, 1989.

Index

Harvard University Press is a member of Green Press Initiative (greenpressinitiative.org), a nonprofit organization working to help publishers and printers increase their use of recycled paper and decrease their use of fiber derived from endangered forests. This book was printed on 100% recycled paper containing 50% post-consumer waste and processed chlorine free.